Ruth & Naomi—
The Healing Journey

Debbye Graafsma, mcc, bcpc

Inner Life Discovery, Recovery & Development

Study Workbook

Awakened!!
Awakened to Grow
Counsel. Classes. Retreats
awakenedtogrow.com

This workbook is curriculum to accompany video sessions 1-12, available through

awakenedtogrow.com

Ruth and Naomi – The Healing Journey
ISBN -- 978-0-9852680-2-2
First edition publish date: August 1, 2012

© 2005. Awakened to Grow Ministries/Debbye Graafsma. All materials contained in this notebook are the creation and property of the author. Reproduction by any means is prohibited without the expressed written consent of the owner. Thank you for your integrity. At printing time, all artwork contained herein was royalty free.

Ruth and Naomi ~ The Healing Journey

Individual Journaling Workbook

written by
Rev. Debbye Graafsma, mcc, bcpc

Ruth & Naomi — The Healing Journey

This workbook is designed to accompany recorded teaching sessions, available through our ministry address, or online at awakenedtogrow.com.

Table of Contents

Welcome and Introduction --- 7

Personal Assignment Notebook -- 16

Session One – Orientation --- 17

Session Two— The Perfect Parent --- 37

Session Three – Grief and its Cycles -- 49

Session Four – Deceptions and Lies -- 63

Session Five – All Knotted Up --- 77

Session Six -- Truth and the Problem with Denial ------------------------------ 91

Session Seven – How Shame Becomes a Template for Living ---------------------- 109

Session Eight – The Composition of a Princess -------------------------------- 123

Session Nine -- The Shaping of Personality ----------------------------------- 138

Session Ten – The Patterns of Safe Community --------------------------------- 154

Session Eleven – Assessing Emotional Development ----------------------------- 167

Session Twelve – Identity Formation -- 175

Ruth & Naomi
- The Healing Journey

Greetings, Dear New Partnership Member!!

If you are reading this section, you have probably just signed up for the Ruth and Naomi Partnership, or are considering becoming a participant in a group beginning in your area. Perhaps you are working through the materials as part of a class in ministry training. Whatever your reason, I pray Abba Father's wisdom & blessing upon you, as you seek to grow in the love and life of our Lord Jesus.

You are headed into an adventure!!

The Ruth and Naomi Partnership is a ministry program which our Women's Ministries offer once a year, in the church my husband, Bill, and I pastor together. The CD lessons, charts and worksheets are a culmination of my experiences as a pastor to women, over the past twenty-some years. And, as it turns out, this has been somewhat of an adventure for me, as well. I never thought I would be working with women, especially in regard to these kinds of issues. (I always thought my field would be limited to teaching piano and leading worship!!) ☺

When Bill and I first began in ministry together, I noticed that the women who seemed drawn to me had a common denominator – brokenness. When it came to worship and teach-ability, that was a good thing… These women were sweet, open, and caring. But none could seem to find the strength to step up into leadership roles, and remain in those offices long-term, without developing a sort of emotional insulation. This insulation, I found, eventually would invite a hardening within each of them to the Presence of God. Spirit-life would become something based on "doing" the right thing – instead of "being" the right person.

And somehow, they felt trapped, forced to continue on "task", many times without joy – or the ability/desire to continue. They also felt drained emotionally.

Then, an inability to express, give, and truly receive unconditional love would also surface, although it certainly had not shown itself before they were given responsibility. Carefulness, and a fear of community (within the Body of Christ!) began to show itself as well.

And, even when I would teach, reassure, counsel, encourage, and spend my own energies to help these women come to a place of consistency and security, there was an underlying brokenness that remained; continually speaking fragility in day-to-day relationships. I found myself increasingly needing to give out more and more, sometimes to the point of parenting women who were older than myself. These precious ladies just couldn't seem to find a handle for their daily life events. They needed help on a human level – and I found myself tempted to "refer them to a professional." But the Holy Spirit kept nudging my heart when I would pray – there was something I was missing in my hurry to "do" women's ministry. And, as I allowed Him to slow my pace, Bill and I began to finally grasp what it means to really disciple another person.

The pathway into true and lasting discipleship could only be entered through the surrender and healing process. Further…. Over the years, we observed the problem was not always demonic in nature. In more than half of these ladies, the problems were emotionally based. That, within the infrastructure of personal development, there simply was no foundation prepared – or reserved stability – to support the weight of relationships and/or tasks long-term. And, beyond responsibilities, the majority of these women had issues with personal vulnerability and trust. Many insulated themselves into a busy life-style, with no connection or real heart-to-heart community – even within a church setting. (Some of these would say "*especially* within a church setting!")

These women just found life difficult.

As our ministry journey has continued, I have learned that initial brokenness in each life, many times has come from a missing link in a woman's personal development. The missing link seems to be the same, no matter what weapon the enemy has used to bring that brokenness about in the first place; whether emotional abuse, neglect, hunger, abandonment, rape, sexual abuse, molestation, alcoholic/addicted environments, divorce, or any number of other armaments in Satan's arsenal. I am also learning that this experience is not just limited to women.

Here are some statistics to help you to see how widespread these situations have become in our culture.

- a. 55%-70% of every church in every ethnicity in the United States consists of women. That means more than half of all congregations are female.

- b. 80% of women feel inadequate to make decisions that affect their own lives and the lives of others on a deep level.

- c. 65% or more of women have some form of dysfunction that they perceive has stymied them in their development to any kind of destiny, perceived or unknown.

- d. 70% of women deal with depression, whether chemical or hormonal, triggered by inner life issues.

- e. 75% or more of women *in the church* have experimented with drugs, alcohol, the occult, or sexual immorality, the scars of which have not been addressed on a deep level.

- f. 3 in 5 or more, of women in the church have experience sexual abuse, physical abuse, or molestation before the age of 15. (We say "or more" because those statistics address the reported cases. The statistic is 1 in 5 for men.)

- g. 85% or more of women have chosen to protect themselves with defensive mechanisms, and hold anger and distrust toward authority figures; living fear, guilt and shame based – with a sense of attachment hunger; being emotionally removed or "left out" in life situations.

- h. 75% or more of women have experienced a negative imprinting of male or female authority, constituted by neglect, ignorance, abandonment, or abuse. Of these, all I have known have determined that their abuse indicated something about their life purpose and value.

i. 55% or more of women have experienced divorce, separation or marriage failure. (Marriage failure occurs when a couple continues to live together without connection; without real love in the marriage.)

j. 63% or more of women have experienced abortion. Of those women in that 63%, more than half have experienced more than one abortion.

And yet,

k. 90% of Protestant churches and 100% of Catholic churches place men in the top leadership roles, with little or no structured ministry in place to help women to deal with their past issues, further reinforcing a fear of trusting male authority in many women. Or, when a man does reach to help a woman with this type of brokenness, he finds himself in a place of sexual and emotional temptation.

l. Approximately 45% of pastoral leadership in the United States targets men for ministry, and down plays the needs of the females in the congregation, as subservient, less important, or worse, "hormonal." The conclusion among many women is that they must just learn to live with the pain they feel. Even Christian women come to believe that the world is a "man's world." (Too often, the only ministry available to women in the church is seen in areas where they are allowed to serve, with nothing specific to address their personal issues.)

m. In the last fifteen years, there has been a 60% decline in church attendance among women who used to attend regularly.

n. 40% or more of Protestant Christian women communicate they feel inadequate to mentor or disciple other women; they lack confidence that what they would share would really help someone – because they are unsure they have learned the right things. And, beyond that, in many lives, "doing the right thing," has replaced "becoming the right person," in their experience. These women struggle with emptiness in their spiritual understanding – going "through the motions" without real joy or substance of Life; without a real and growing *relationship* with Jesus Christ.

What is the missing link? On a spiritual level, it is the absence of real and transforming spiritual power in our church environments. On a human level, it is *the ability to truly bond with another human being*; the ability to give one's heart to another person, without reserve – without fear; without waiting for the "other shoe to drop," or "keeping your options open, just in case." And, the need for mentoring and what I have come to call "Gap Parenting," is even greater. It is a deep need for the Creator's Community; for relationship; for discipling; for unconditional friendship.

Sometimes, the ability to bond has been present in early childhood, but has been broken by trauma. Sometimes, and sadly, what I have found to be more common, the bond was never present to begin with. Consider these personal accounts, from women I have worked with over the years –

- She was a latch-key kid, raised in a Christian home, by working parents, who were never emotionally available. She couldn't remember a time when she felt connected, even though she had always gone to church. Even now, she has few friends, even though she tries to be a nice person. She finds it difficult to trust other women with the issues closest to her heart.

- She hadn't realized until she experienced the program; and wouldn't have thought there were gaps in her emotional development. She had managed to get through the hard years of rejection in school, and the gangly years without knowing what to do when the kids made fun of her. But now, she can't seem to even force herself to become part of a group, without having to be in control of its direction in some way.

- Her father was mentally ill, and her mother would bring "uncles" home, allowing her three year old daughter to witness sexual acts that should never be seen, even by adults.

- Her mother and her mother's boyfriend didn't want the children "stealing food," so they put a lock and chain around the refrigerator. The parents spent their time locked in the bedroom, sometimes with friends. The six-year old girl, and her four-year old brother, would dig in the garbage for their parents' scraps, and fall asleep on the floor whenever they became tired, without a blanket, or pillow, or comfort. She remembers television being a constant companion.

- Her father and mother just were never there, and she chose to fend for herself and her baby brother at the age of five. She remembers cooking and cleaning, changing diapers and washing clothes when she made this decision. Now, she finds it difficult to stop working and allow herself to enjoy the relationships God has provided in the people around her.

- Her father sodomized her and threw her out of the house when she was 16, without clothing or money, because she had expressed a desire to go to college. She struggled with a homosexual life-style for over 5 years.

- Her alcoholic father beat her when she told him she was hungry. Then, she and her hungry siblings were forced to stand and watch him, as he consumed a steak dinner.

- Her husband would keep her at home without a vehicle, control her activities, and expect sex each night. When she was too tired to give it to him, after caring for her two toddlers during the day, as well as a neighbor's child, he would rape her. He expected an account for her wages, her time, and even her telephone calls. This abuse was spiritualized, in the name of "godly submission."

There are so many other stories – perhaps yours is similar to ones I have just given. If that is the case, you need to know that God never wanted you to be treated in this way – He places more value on your life than other people have.

Know this: Jesus is still in the healing business – and He knows exactly where you are – and what you need in order to come into deeper relationship with Him. He is preparing you for an eternal purpose – and He is doing that preparation right now.

Perhaps you have felt powerless in your ability to move beyond the level of spiritual life you have been experiencing. This book and the group ministry of the Partnership will help you to discover key areas where you have become "stuck," or decided to just "quit hoping for more."

But you didn't really quit -- now you are considering another step.

Any step you take will involve growth. And growth will always involve healing. After all, the root word in "healthy" is "heal." So, any journey into emotional and spiritual wholeness, will involve some sort of change – because growth cannot happen without change – just look at children's student pictures from one year to the next. So, growth is healing, and healing means change.

And isn't that what you are really hungry for? A safe and solid change?

Consider too; *everyone on the planet is broken* – No one has "arrived." Additionally, none of us have the ability to heal ourselves. So know this, you are not alone in this place where you are.

Let me tell you how the Ruth and Naomi Partnership came into being:

In 2002, I found myself working with a woman who has since become a dear friend. In the process of helping her to untangle the confusion caused by abuse, we began working toward the healing of broken trust. We also began addressing issues of personal identity formation. I began going back through my ministry journals, in the process of developing worksheets for her. The idea was to help her to understand the nature of Father God – that He is Abba – and unlike any other male or female authority figure she had ever known.

I had taught these materials before. Bill and I had developed workbooks for Inner Life Development, as part of a program we had written several years prior, called "Lessons for Liberty." Part One of this study was entitled, "Everyone Needs a Dad." Usually, the Lord would have me just incorporate new ladies into that program. But this time, for this woman, the Holy Spirit kept leading me to create worksheets just for her, which would cause her to "dig it out" for herself, and would target her key areas of pain. We ended up going an entirely different direction than I anticipated.

It took us a little over a year.

At the end of that year, several other women, who knew of her struggles and subsequent victories, *(and who, unknown to me, had been watching to see if she had experienced breakthrough),* asked if they could have the same worksheets for their own use. Upon presenting the idea to our entire women's ministry, we had more than twenty come to the orientation session. That was almost a third of our women! I was overwhelmed. It would be impossible to mentor one-on-one with twenty some ladies!

So, we decided to try a group. I told them they would be part of an experiment; that we were developing a concept, and I was only seeing one step at a time. They didn't mind. They *wanted* to do the work no matter what it meant. They were hungry, and ready for help. Incidentally, that attitude, I have found, is one of the main and necessary ingredients for a person to experience healing on any level.

We kept our first session of the partnership open-ended, just because we didn't know how long it would take to get all the ladies through the program. And also because of two key principles I have learned in ministry:

1. Maturity cannot be rushed, and
2. Discovery cannot be forced.

For more than thirty years, in helping people develop inner life, I have been a firm believer in having a person sign a commitment for their own growth, so we developed a "Covenant Agreement," knowing that the Agreement would serve as a reminder of the Lord's promises to heal and seal His work in our lives, later when the path became painful for those involved. We also felt we needed some "Pillar Principles" for the ladies to agree to, so we could build unity and a sense of ownership within the group.

We found ourselves continually coming back to these principles, in counseling between sessions, and in encouraging each other when Pain became the most strident voice within the soul. The Principles are:

1. I choose to move forward
2. I choose to serve
3. I choose to be a safe person
4. I choose to allow others into my life.

It is my deepest hope that as you work through these materials, that the Presence of Jesus and His Holy Spirit, will visit you, envelope you, strengthen and encourage you, breathe upon you, and heal your life.

He is the Healer. He is the Restorer.
He is always Trustworthy.

He loves you. And so do I.

Blessings on your journey!!

Debbye Graafsma

Ruth & Naomi

Personal Assignment Workbook

Please utilize these note pages as you listen to the recorded lecture for Session One.

Ruth and Naomi – The Healing Journey
Session One – Orientation

1. What is the purpose of the Ruth and Naomi Ministry?

2. What will happen as I participate in this group?

3. How will incorporating the Covenant Agreement into my life approach for growth help me to realize personal growth and emotional development?

4. What focus will emerge as we walk through the materials together?

Levels of Communication

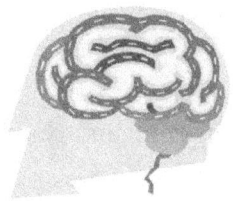

1. Clichés

2. Facts

IQ   Outer Life

Task & Doing

IMAGE BASED

Tangible

Wall of self protection—pride+fear=control

Inner Life

Intangible

3. Principles/Values/Morals Feelings

4. Yearnings/Needs

EQ

Relationship & Being

TRUTH BASED

Line of selfless choice

IQ & EQ   5. Deep sense of security & approval/Child

OBEDIENCE BASED

© dg atg

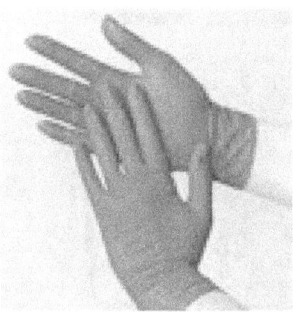 What does God look at first, when He looks at me?

 The Iceberg Principle of Emotional Intelligence

Assessment

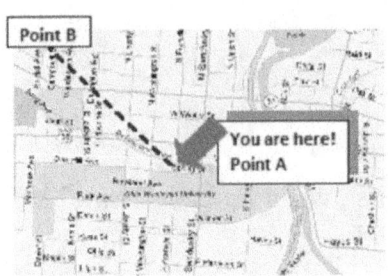

Point B – Health
Point A – Present Location

Before a pathway can be charted to a final destination of health and development, we must assess or appraise where we are presently living. Without a proper appraisal, it is impossible to map out a straight line; creating personal application of the need for growth.

Results:
Truth/reality speaks
Emotional awareness
Healing of memories
Grief is processed
Facilitates growth and healing

Judgment

Good or Bad
Pass or Fail
Right or Wrong
Win or Lose

Judgment attaches a *negative moral value* to the "You are Here" mechanism and closes the gate to growth/change.

Results:
Negative emotions speak/control
Numbness of heart
Repressed memories
Stalled grief cycle
Stops growth and healing

© atg/dcg

Notes:

Assessment

"GOD IS MY HEALER AND FRIEND"

Abba Father views us through the eyes of assessment, seeing our places of pain as potential meeting places for comfort and healing.

Elements of Assessment

1. Assigns value to people because they carry the image of God within themselves – either with Jesus or without Him.
2. Operates through a heart choice of love, trust, community, and mutual safety.
3. Uses potential and relationship to motivate; Holy Spirit led, serving based; Kingdom order.
4. What a person does flows from who they are becoming
5. Weakness and mistakes are expected elements of learning
6. Abba Father based, relationship centered
7. Acceptance and approval are centered in the unconditional and unfailing love of God—all are equal.

Judgment

"GOD IS A HARD MAN, WAITING FOR ME TO MESS UP"

We view ourselves through the eyes of judgment, seeing our places of pain as places of potential rejection, disapproval and ultimate rejection by God.

Elements of Judgment

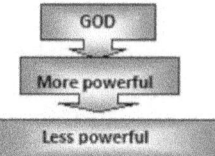

1. Assigns value to people based upon beauty, achievement, Success, health, brains, and ability
2. Operates through a mindset of authority, hierarchy, politicism, religious traditions & institutional organization.
3. Uses fear to motivate; performance driven; man's order
4. What a person does is more important than who they are
5. Weakness and mistakes diminish value /unacceptable
6. Man based; Rules centered
7. Rejection and disapproval of those who are different than Common group

© atg/dcg

Notes:

Session One – Homework

1. Please fill out the Personal Assessment, as well as the "How Do I See Myself?" evaluation on the pages which follow this page. You will need to give these to your Partnership Facilitator at the beginning of the next session. She will keep these materials confidential.

2. Please read and complete the Ruth and Naomi Covenant Agreement, as well as the requested library book list. Please save the *second signed sheet* to give to your Partnership Facilitator at the next session.

3. Please complete the worksheets in the Personal Discovery Journal section for this Session.

4. Before the next session, please read Psalm 23 each day, perhaps just before bedtime, and ask Jesus to show you one specific way in which He is your personal Shepherd.

Personal Assessment Sheet – Session One
(all answers are confidential and will not be shared)

1. What is your personal goal in coming to this group? (If you don't have one, its okay to say, I don't know.)

2. Are there personal relationships in your life at the present time that you would like to have a better handle on? Which ones are they, and why?

3. What issues would you like to be better equipped to address in your personal life with Jesus?

How Do I See Myself?   Name/Date:

Please use the scales provided to answer the following questions. It is helpful if you take a few moments with each question, and consider your "heart" answer, rather than giving a quick "head" answer. In this way, you will be able to obtain a clearer reading of the state of your soul's health .

Please rate the answer to each question, by circling a number/indicator.

1. **Am I happy with my life?**

Ecstatic & Thrilled				Content/Happy			Discouraged/Miserable			
10	9	8	7	6	5	4	3	2	1	0

What causes you to respond with this answer? What evidences are present in your life to support your response?

_____

_____

_____

_____

2. **Do people really like me?**

I have several relationships which bring value				My presence in most situations is just tolerated			Not really. What's to like about me?			
10	9	8	7	6	5	4	3	2	1	0

What causes you to respond with this answer? What evidences are present in your life to support your response?

_____

_____

3. Do I look acceptable?

| I am stunning | My looks are acceptable for my age and life experience | I have several physical attributes which I really don't like. | I hate the way I look. |

10   9   8   7   6   5   4   3   2   1   0

What causes you to respond with this answer? What evidences are present in your life to support your response?

_____

_____

4. Does my family love me?

| I am an unreplaceable member of an inseparable family community | I fulfill a function as a caregiver | I feel drained of resource most of the time | I have no one to really care for me, but I give continually |

10   9   8   7   6   5   4   3   2   1   0

What causes you to respond with this answer? What evidences are present in your life to support your response?

_____

_____

_____

5. Do I feel as though I have something to contribute to others?

I have an un-replaceable contribution to the lives I touch every day.	I feel reasonably satisfied that my life makes a difference.	I fulfill a function, but it's something anyone else could do.	I am only tolerated in presence and in contribution

10   9   8   7   6   5   4   3   2   1   0

What causes you to respond with this answer? What evidences are present in your life to support your response?

_____

_____

_____

_____

6. Do I feel I am responsible to maintain the emotional state of those I care for?

They are responsible for their choices, and I am free from feelings of negativity.	I seek to live my life aware of their needs, but I don't try to "create" an optimum environment.	I am responsible for my family's (or friends) unhappiness, and I must see that the atmosphere in our lives is a happy one.	I live in fear of someone's anger or negativity, and I try to condition my life to avoid those responses.

10   9   8   7   6   5   4   3   2   1   0

What causes you to respond with this answer? What evidences are present in your life to support your response?

_____

_____

7. Do I think Father God loves me?

| I experience His love and relationship every day | I know He does, but I don't feel anything. | How can He love me? Look at my life. | He doesn't care, and I don't either. |

10   9   8   7   6   5   4   3   2   1   0

What causes you to respond with this answer? What evidences are present in your life to support your response?

_____

_____

_____

_____

Ruth & Naomi Women's Ministry — The Healing Journey

Covenant Agreement

In a desire to grow in my inner life, I covenant with the Holy Spirit, and those I am accountable to in this process, to enter into this learning relationship. In obedience to the Word of God, I choose to receive development through this process.

In entering into this new relationship, I acknowledge the following growth desires to be true for my life:

1. I desire to leave my past behind me, and enter into a new place

2. I desire to grow in my identity as a woman of God, learning from those the Father has placed in my life for instruction.

3. I desire to serve well, and finish well.

4. I desire to develop a larger heart, capable of mentoring other women in Spirit-formed development.

5. I desire to apply the Word of God to my life, not just mentally, but in practice.

6. I desire to be a contributing servant in every area of my life; physically, spiritually, and emotionally.

7. I desire to live my life as a life-long learner, and understand this mentoring program/process is a walking out of that desire.

Page two – Ruth & Naomi -- The Healing Journey --

In beginning this new phase of spiritual discipleship, I choose to commit to the following principles of practice for the Ruth and Naomi -- The Healing Journey.

1. I choose to leave the past behind.   (Ruth 1:6)

2. I choose to cling to the new thing Jesus is doing in my life.   (Ruth 1:14)

3. I determine to receive a new identity and genetic makeup, based upon the Word of God., according to the Holy Spirit's leading in my own heart.   (Ruth 1:16)

4. I choose to serve in practical ways as I grow.   (Ruth 2:12)

5. I understand that redemption and spiritual covering are the purpose-directed pillars of this mentoring ministry. I choose to follow instructions for spiritual and emotional growth and development, as they are provided for me, through assignments and relational communication.   (Ruth 3:1-15)

6. I choose to keep my heart open and teachable in this process of development. I choose to trust. It is my desire to recognize excellence Father has placed within the other women in this group. I choose to value their participation in this group as well as my own. I will complete my assignments.

7. I open my heart to my Kinsman-Redeemer, **Jesus**; Who loves me, and will spread His Covering of Grace over my heart and life as I step into the new places He is preparing for me in this process.

Page three – Ruth & Naomi -- The Healing Journey

As a participant in the Ruth and Naomi Ministry, I acknowledge and agree to the following:

1. I will seek to set the four tenet principles of the Ruth and Naomi Ministry into the fabric of my daily life:
    a. "I choose to move forward."
    (This prevents me from becoming "stuck.")

    b. "I choose to serve."
    (This prevents me from becoming self-centered and selfish in the healing process. It confronts any narcissism, or tendency to become self-absorbed.)

    c. "I choose to become a safe person."
    (This protects me from either violating my relationships with other women, and provides a net of safety for myself, as I develop trust in areas of relational connection with other women. We will create a safe place together.)

    d.. "I choose to allow others into my life."
    (These prevent me from becoming a "lone ranger," and draws me into fellowship with other women. Community will become a positive in my life, replacing the negative concept I have had until now.)

2. I will listen to and apply the teaching from each session's CD, to the best of my ability and understanding. I will complete the assignments in the Ruth and Naomi workbook.

3. I will attend all of the sessions, unless I have an emergency or crisis which demands my attendance. I will set time aside to feed my soul, and to grow in the things of Christ- based spiritual life.

4. If I choose not to complete the materials, I understand that I will move to an audit status, and it will prevent me from being able to be utilized as a ministry partner for other women in need. In order to be placed in a ministry capacity, I need to complete all of the materials, and apply them to my life.

5. I agree to read the supplemental reading books. If I would like to read additional books, I can choose from the provided book list.

6. I understand that I may indicate my preference to share or not to share in regard to personal needs while in the Ruth and Naomi program. However, I do desire to develop a deeper ability to trust and relate to others. Realizing this, I want to try to learn to trust others within a safe environment. I will then become able to experience the stretching of my personal trust levels in groups outside of this group of women. This group is a safe place for me. I choose to allow it to be so. For my part, I will be a safe person for other women in this group. If I violate confidentiality within this place of trust, by sharing "out of school" I understand that I am discarding the privilege of participation.

Additional Supplemental Reading List:

Required Texts:
    "Journey"   by Debbye Graafsma
    "The Divine Romance"   by Gene Edwards
    "The Blood"   by Benny Hinn
    "The Mom Factor"   by Henry Cloud and John Townsend

Additional Available Recommended Texts *(and their subject matter)*

    "Into Abba's Arms" by Sandra Wilson, PhD. *(how to develop a love life with God)*

    "Control Freak" by Les Parrott, PhD *(how to learn to trust and let go of control)*

    "The World's Easiest Guide to Family Relationships" by Gary Chapman
(explains what healthy family life should look like)

    "Door of Hope" by Jan Frank
(how to make the journey out of the pain of sexual abuse and incest)

    "The Lies We Believe" by Chris Thurman
(how to learn to believe truth, and not what your emotions have been programmed to believe, by experiences and relational histories)

    "Released from Shame" by Sandra Wilson PhD
(how to experience freedom from the heaviness that false guilt and shame carry)

    "Making Anger Your Ally" by Dr. Neil Clark Warren
(practical approaches to dealing with the problem of Anger)

    "High Maintenance Relationships" by Les Parrott
(what is really going on inside the difficult people in your life, and how you can relate to them more easily)

    "Love's Unseen Enemy" by Les Parrot
(learning what a relationship built on unconditional love looks like, and how each of us have been influenced by guilt, to settle for counterfeit methods of love, ie, pleasing, controlling, with-holding, etc.)

    "Safe People" by Cloud and Townsend
(How the processes of disaffection destroy our abilities to have long-term romantic relationships, how they destroy a marriage, and how to break the cycle.)

    "Loving People" by Cloud and Townsend
(How to learn to experience emotional intimacy with others, without sexual confusion. A really good book for those who would like to learn to bond in relationships.)

Please sign both agreements sheets. Keep one in your notebook, and hand one in at the next session.

I have read the ministry covenant agreement, and I agree to abide by its principles.

Participant _____

Date _____

I would like to read additional supplemental books: (please indicate which ones- we will try to make them available through a lending library)

_____ "Journey" by Debbye Graafsma

_____ "Into Abba's Arms" by Sandra Wilson

_____ "Control Freak" by Les Parrott

_____ "The World's Easiest Guide to Family Relationships" by Gary Chapman

_____ "Door of Hope" by Jan Frank

_____ "The Lies We Believe" by Chris Thurman

_____ "Released from Shame" by Sandra Wilson PhD

_____ "Making Anger Your Ally" by Dr. Neil Clark Warren

_____ "High Maintenance Relationships" by Les Parrott

_____ "Love's Unseen Enemy" by Les Parrott

_____ "Safe People" by Cloud and Townsend

_____ "Loving People" by John Trent

(Please give this copy to the Partnership Facilitator)

I have read the ministry covenant agreement, and I agree to abide by its principles.

Participant _____

Date _____

I would like to read additional supplemental books: (please indicate which ones- we will try to make them available through a lending library)

_____ "Journey" by Debbye Graafsma

_____ "Into Abba's Arms" by Sandra Wilson

_____ "Control Freak" by Les Parrott

_____ "The World's Easiest Guide to Family Relationships" by Gary Chapman

_____ "Door of Hope" by Jan Frank

_____ "The Lies We Believe" by Chris Thurman

_____ "Released from Shame" by Sandra Wilson PhD

_____ "Making Anger Your Ally" by Dr. Neil Clark Warren

_____ "High Maintenance Relationships" by Les Parrott

_____ "Love's Unseen Enemy" by Les Parrott

_____ "Safe People" by Cloud and Townsend

_____ "Loving People" by John Trent

Session One ~
Personal Discovery Journal

Mentoring Assignment #1
Identifying the Attributes of Abba Father

1. As we begin this journey toward whole-ness of soul, it important that we first establish a healthy understanding of what it means to maintain a healthy relationship with our Creator. The Bible refers to God as a Father, so for each of us, He has become the Ultimate Authority Figure in all of our lives – Father God. For some women, it is difficult to approach God at all, because He is presented as a male authority figure. Many of us deal with broken images of male authority, because earthly men have misrepresented Father in our lives. For some of us, the word "father" is a dirty word. For some, it calls to images of abuse and harshness. Whatever the response to the word, "father," each of us have areas where the correct understanding of male authority has been altered from our Creator's original plan. So, as we begin this process of healing, it is important we first gain an unfiltered grasp of just exactly *Who* it is we are dealing with, when we approach Father God.

    In every life, there exists a filter, created by our perceptions and imprinting at our earliest stages of development. In this ministry, we refer to this filter as the "father filter." By definition, it means, that every person on the planet filters their perception of their Heavenly Father, through their perception of their earthly father. And, subsequently, what we perceive to be normal occurrences in our lives as children becomes the basis for how we approach life as adults.

Utilizing the following scriptures, please list out the characteristics of Father God provided for our understanding in the Word.

Scripture	Attribute
Luke 1:37 "For with God nothing will be impossible."	
Psalm 34:8	
Psalm 86:15 "But You, O Lord, *are* a God full of compassion, and gracious, Longsuffering and abundant in mercy and truth."	
Hebrews 13:8	
James 1:17 "Every good gift and every perfect gift is from above, and comes down from the Father of lights, with whom there is no variation or shadow of turning."	
Hebrews 6:18	
Numbers 23:19 "God *is* not a man, that He should lie, Nor a son of man, that He should repent. Has He said, and will He not do? Or has He spoken, and will He not make it good?	
I John 1:9	
Isaiah 43:25 "I, *even* I, *am* He who blots out your transgressions for My own sake; and I will not remember your sins."	
Jeremiah 31:34	
I John 4:7-8	
Psalm 139:13-16	
Genesis 12:1-3 Galatians 3:7-9	

Scripture	Attribute

Psalm 103:3-5 "Who forgives all your iniquities, Who heals all your diseases, Who redeems your life from destruction, Who crowns you with lovingkindness and tender mercies, Who satisfies your mouth with good *things* *So that* your youth is renewed like the eagle's."

Psalm 103:10-11

Psalm 103:17

Luke 11:9-13 "So I say to you, ask, and it will be given to you; seek, and you will find; knock, and it will be opened to you. For everyone who asks receives, and he who seeks finds, and to him who knocks it will be opened. If a son asks for bread from any father among you, will he give him a stone? Or if *he asks* for a fish, will he give him a serpent instead of a fish? Or if he asks for an egg, will he offer him a scorpion? If you then, being evil, know how to give good gifts to your children, how much more will *your* heavenly Father give the Holy Spirit to those who ask Him!"

Exodus 15:2
II Corinthians 12:9

II Peter 3:9

<u>Please utilize these note pages as you listen to the recorded lecture for Session Two.</u>

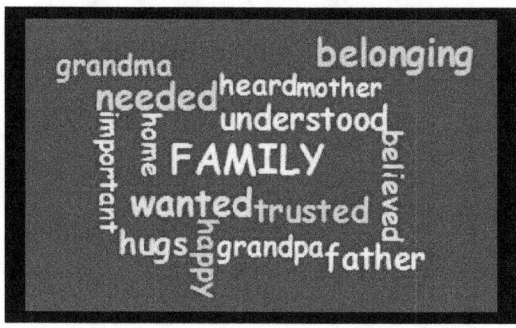

Ruth and Naomi – The Healing Journey
Session Two – "The Perfect Parent"

Romans 8:15

Galatians 4:4-7

Ephesians 1:3-7

The Problem with Living a "Filtered" Life.

What are my current filters?

What fears flavor my understanding of who God is?

Adoptive Bonding Steps
Instructions for adoptive parents

Bonding with an adopted child is not really that difficult. However, it does take intentional effort. The level of difficulty in bonding varies, depending on the child's age and past experiences during foster care or with the biological parents. The child's deepest need is unconditional love, and it is important to remember above all else, especially in the beginning of the bonding process, to remain focused upon providing a safe, stable, and supportive home – no matter how distant or upset they may be seem.

<u>Spiritual and emotional metaphor
in Abba's Personality</u>

1. Clear your schedule, creating as much one-on-one time as possible. The younger the child, the more important it is minimize distractions.

2. Meet the child's basic needs (feeding, changing, comforting when scared or upset, etc) quickly and fully. Show your child that you are someone who can be trusted to take care of them. Building trust is the first foundation stone in creating a bonding relationship.

3. It is important to spend quantity time being physically accessible to your child. Cuddle with them. Lots of safe touch is a key. Plan activities that encourage eye contact. Sharing smiles and games will also help you to develop common ground and happy memories together.

4. Consider co-sleeping to promote additional closeness and allow you to meet any needs that arise in the night. An adopted child is often scared and uncertain at night and having Mom or Dad close by can help a great deal.

5. Allow your child time to grieve the loss of their former caregivers or her birth parents. Even an infant can sense when things are different. It is important the child be allowed and helped to grieve that loss. An older child will often struggle with feelings of helplessness -- not understanding what has happened. Be patient. Allow the child to process any negative feelings. This will help a great deal towards developing a healthy bond between you.

6. Be patient. Realize that bonding takes time. If you don't instantly fall in love with your child it doesn't mean there is anything wrong. Sometimes that feeling of love and affection will come right away but often it takes time to feel a connection. Give it time and try to enjoy the process of becoming a truly bonded family.

7. Don't force your love or affections onto the child. Let them know that you are there for them and that you would like to spend time with them.

8. Give your child personal space to spend time in. Respect that space as their own. Always knock on the door before entering, and no matter how much you may dislike it, allow them to decorate and paint (or help them paint, etc.) the room so that it is their "Own" space. They need to feel that the new home is their own and that they can feel comfortable staying there.

9. If your child is a different or nationality than you, respect it. Ask your child if they would like to celebrate certain holidays or parts of their heritage, and be open to learning about them. Ask the child if they can help you to learn about the religion or heritage/celebration. Go to the library or search online about what is involved and have the child show you what they know about it. It may not be part of what you consider "the holidays" but it will need to be from now on. Even if the child doesn't speak up about it, you still need to ask if they would like to celebrate or learn about it. Otherwise- resentment may quietly build.

10. Ask questions but don't pry. Talk about their past in an open way. NEVER try to hide the fact or forget the fact that they were adopted. Staying open and honest will make them trust you and will turn you into "mom or dad" faster than lying or faking it ever would.

11. Let the child have some control over the family choices. Let them choose a family dinner each night, a family activity each week, a game you play, or a movie you see. They need to have a little bit of control in a life that has previously been so out of their control.

12. Never put down or attack the biological parent's character. Even if they gave the child up for adoption for horrible reasons and even if you disagree with their lifestyle, etc. NEVER tell the child that the biological parents were "bad" or "worthless" etc. No good can come of this- it will only reflect badly upon you in the long run.

13. Relax. The relationship will build with time. As the child begins to see that you respect and care about them, then love will grow. They will slowly begin to see you as "mom or dad" and their early life will become less important as they become involved in school, sports, etc. Just try and be an open and honest parent, and everything will work out fine!

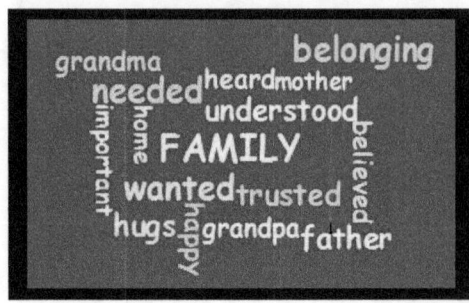

Human Core Desires
For Healthy Relationships

(Bonding)

1. To be noticed
2. To be complimented

Being "normal"

IQ

3. To be recognized/observed
4. To be included
5. To be physically safe
6. To be affirmed/accepted

To "Matter"

~~~~~~~~~~~~~~~~~~~~~~~~~~~~~~~~~~~~

7. To be touched (safely)
8. To be heard (to connect)
9. To belong (in a group)
10. To be received

Holding a needed place
as part of a group

EQ

11. To be trusted
12. To be chosen
13. To be understood (to reciprocate connect)
14. To be integrated into a group

Feeling at home anywhere

~~~~~~~~~~~~~~~~~~~~~~~~~~~~~~~~~~~~

15. To be secure
16. To be preferred
17. To be passionately wanted

Knowing inner safety
even in vulnerability

Core

Copyright 2007, awakened to grow, dcg.

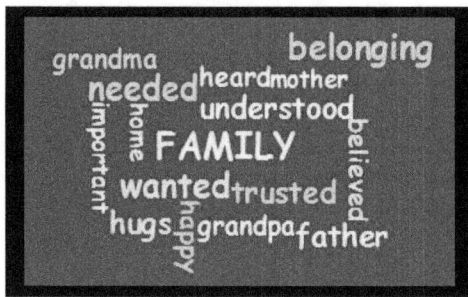

Human Core Desires
For Healthy Relationships

(Abba's Provision as our Adoptive Father)

    1. To be noticed   I Samuel 16:7
    2. To be complimented   Ephesians 4:32

    3. To be seen   Genesis 16:6-13
    4. To be included   Ephesians 2:1-10
    5. To be secure   Psalm 62:8
    6. To be affirmed   Psalm 116:1-9

~~~~~~

    7. To be touched (safely)   Luke 4:18/ Ps. 147:3
    8. To be heard (to connect)   Isaiah 1:18
    9. To belong (in a group)   Psalm 116:1-9
    10. To be received   Psalm 34:15

    11. To be trusted   James 2:23/Ex 33:11
    12. To be chosen   Jeremiah 31:3
    13. To be understood (to reciprocate connect)   Psalm 139
    14. To be integrated   Ephesians 1:6

~~~~~~

    15. To be secure   Psalm 103:8-12/Ps. 18:6-19
    16. To be preferred   John 15:15
    17. To be passionately wanted   Ephesians 1:3-5

© atg/dg.

Session Two – Homework

1. Please gather several pictures of yourself during your childhood. Please make photocopies of these pictures, with one picture on each page. On each page, make a note of your age in each picture. Please place these pages in your notebook.

2. Please take some time before the next session, to journal the story of your life to this point. Make a list of the highlights in telling your story.... Don't use lots of detail unless you feel it will be helpful to get it out on paper. Sometimes, if you have a memory that brings pain to mind, it is good to remember the detail – that will help when we are walking through the healing process later.

    Note: Don't be concerned if painful memories do come to mind... It is usually the instances in our lives that have caused us the most pain which tend to surface – these experiences give us clues as to where and when our emotional development slowed or stopped.

3. Please begin reading the first recommended reading book: "Journey" by Debbye Graafsma, or, if you have finished this book, another supplemental book of your choosing from the required or supplemental reading list.

4. Please memorize the scripture verse: Jeremiah 29:11. "For I know the plans I have towards you," says the Lord; plans for good and not for evil; plans for a future and a hope."

5. Please also take time to read Ephesians, chapters one and two this week each day, preferably at bedtime.

Session Two –
Personal Discovery Journal

Mentoring Assignment #2
Identifying the Attributes of God, Part 2

1. As we continue this journey toward whole-ness of soul, take a few moments to finish the next portion in the journaling exercise we began in Session One. To review, for some women, it is difficult to approach God at all, because He is presented as a male authority figure.

   Many of us deal with broken images of male authority, because earthly men have misrepresented Father in our lives. For some of us, the word "father" is a dirty word. For some, it calls to images of abuse and harshness.

   Whatever the response to the word, "father," each of us have areas where the correct understanding of male authority has been altered from the Creator's original plan, and has created a filter in our lives.

   So, as we begin this process of healing, it is important that we gain an *unfiltered* grasp of just exactly Who we are dealing with, when we approach Father God.

   Please continue the exercise we began last session on the following pages.

Scripture	Attribute
John 6:40 "And this is the will of Him who sent Me, that everyone who sees the Son and believes in Him may have everlasting life; and I will raise him up at the last day."	
Deuteronomy 28:1-13	
John 10:10 "The thief does not come except to steal, and to kill, and to destroy. I have come that they may have life, and that they may have *it* more abundantly."	
Psalm 9:9-10 "The LORD also will be a refuge for the oppressed, A refuge in times of trouble. And those who know Your name will put their trust in You; For You, LORD, have not forsaken those who seek You.	
Hebrews 13:5	
Psalm 28:7 "The LORD *is* my strength and my shield; My heart trusted in Him, and I am helped; Therefore my heart greatly rejoices, And with my song I will praise Him."	
Psalm 31:20	

Scripture	Attribute
Hebrews 13:5-6 "For He Himself has said, *"I will never leave you nor forsake you."* So we may boldly say: *" The LORD is my helper; I will not fear. What can man do to me?"*	
Psalm 18	
Psalm 103:13 "As a father pities *his* children, *So* the LORD pities those who fear Him.	
Psalm 84:11-12	
Philippians 4:19 "And my God shall supply all your need according to His riches in glory by Christ Jesus.	
I John 1:7 "But if we walk in the light as He is in the light, we have fellowship with one another, and the blood of Jesus Christ His Son cleanses us from all sin."	
Psalm 118:6	

Discoveries I made this week:

Please utilize these note pages as you listen to the recorded lecture for Session Three.

Ruth and Naomi – The Healing Journey
Session Three – Grief and Its Cycles

The Principles of Change

1. There is always hope for change.

2. We cannot change what we do not acknowledge.

3. The primary ingredient of the change process is Truth (in love) in an open heart.

4. We cannot change others. We can only change ourselves.

5. Repentance is the only catalyst (beginning place) for change to occur.

6. Our inner brokenness is the beginning place for repentance, and therefore Change.

7. Changes we seek to make within ourselves without the help of the Holy Spirit, will never be permanent, because they are based in our own works and effort.

8. We cannot expect God to give grace or healing, when we are unwilling to repent.

9. Growth cannot happen without change.

10. Change will involve both forward and backward motion, always with our eyes fixed upon the goal of becoming like Christ.

11. The Doorway into the Change Process is guarded from the inside, by a person who must open the door from the inside. It cannot be forced open.

12. Change must be chosen, sometimes with struggle.

13. Change comes as a result of Training, not as a result of simply trying, using the same tools we have used in the past.

14. Change is a process. It takes time. What took years to tear down will require a season of hard work to redeem, repair and restore.

15. It takes intentional maintenance for change to remain.

© atg/dg

BODY
Vehicle for real person (vessel) seeing, hearing, smelling, touching, tasting

SOUL
Mind, will and emotions

SPIRIT
Intuition, communion, inner conscience

© atg/dg

Levels of Communication

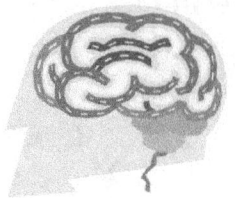

1. Clichés

2. Facts

IQ   Outer Life

Task & Doing

IMAGE BASED

Tangible

Wall of self protection—pride+fear=control

Inner Life

Intangible

3. Principles/Values/Morals Feelings

4. Yearnings/Needs

EQ

Relationship & Being

TRUTH BASED

Line of selfless choice

IQ & EQ   5. Deep sense of security & approval/Child

OBEDIENCE BASED

© dg atg

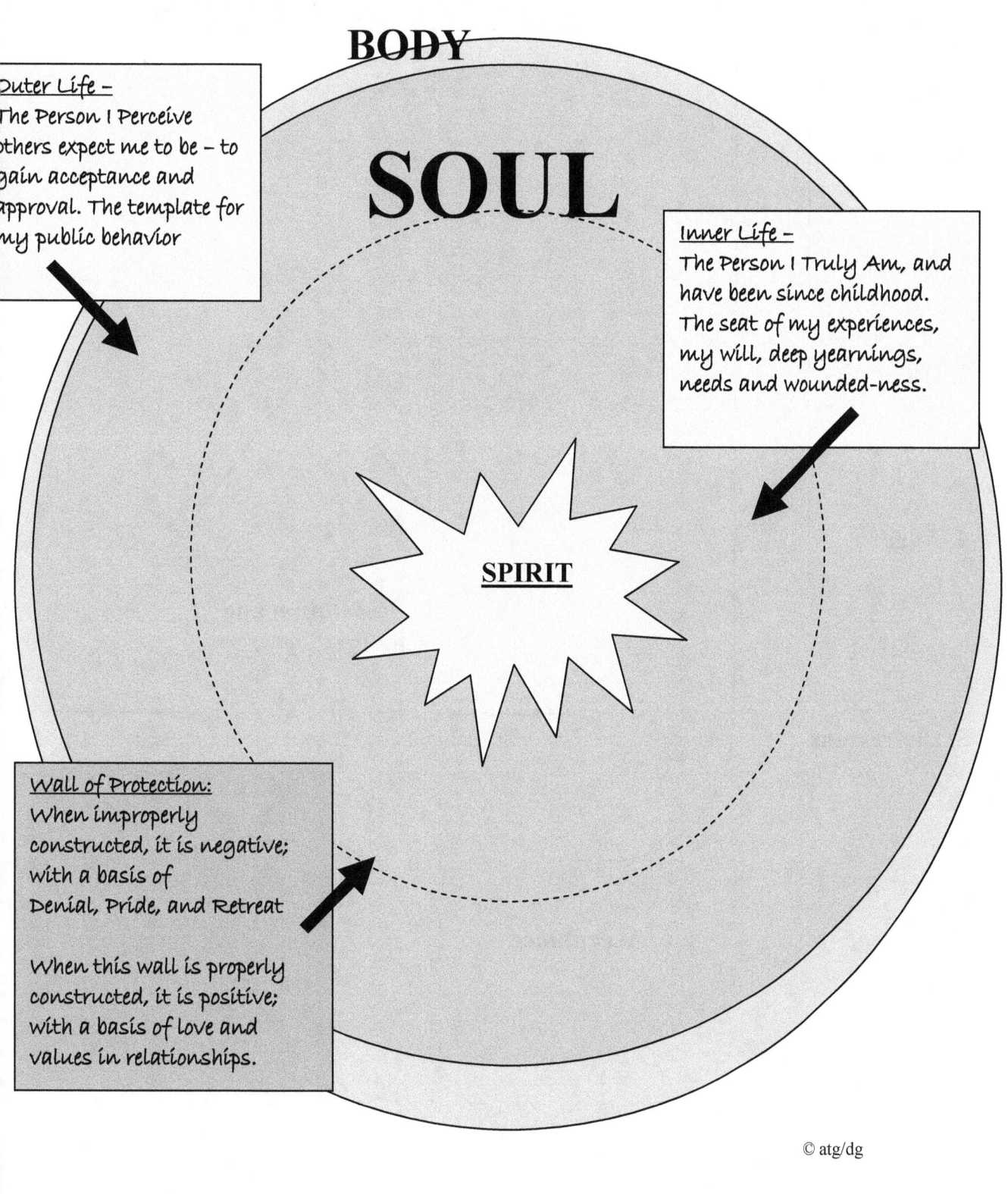

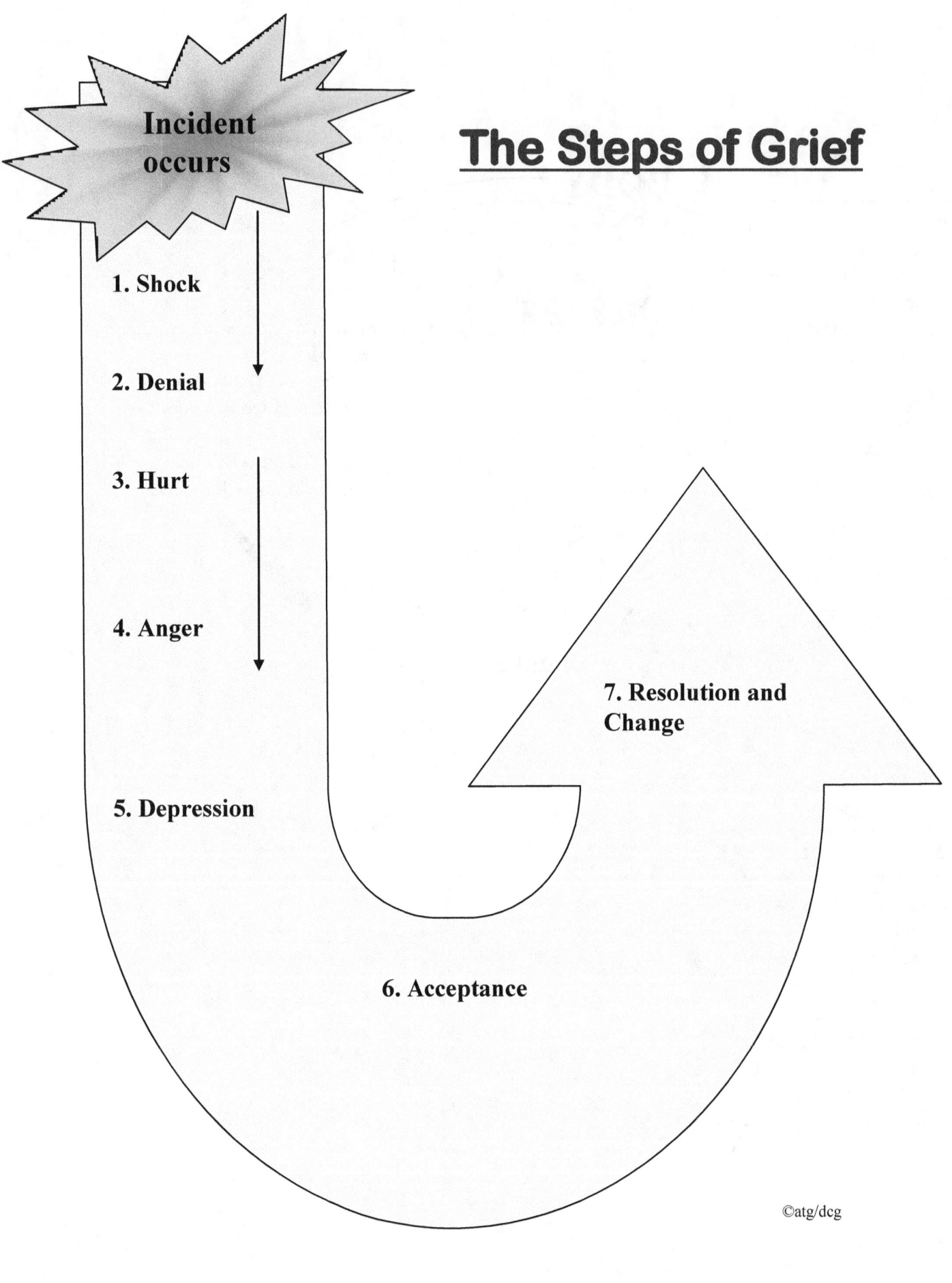

Cyclic pattern Of Stalled Grief

DENIAL'S PING PONG EFFECT

1. blaming
2. placing all fault
3. protesting (justice)
4. control (I'll fix it)
5. manipulation
6. bargaining (mental or action)
7. compensating (approval mechanism)
8. minimalizing
9. rationalizing
10. "spiritualizing" – gloss
11. Religiosity
12. fragmentation
13. detachment
14. withdrawal/retreat
15. addictions
16. coping
17. self-defense
18. Intense emotional responses

DENIAL

DEPRESSION

CAUSES/FORMS OF DEPRESSION

1. clinical depression
2. bi-polar
3. various phobias
4. conduct disorders
5. manic depression
6. schizophrenia
7. passive aggression

HURT

- Takes everything personally
- Centralizes situations back to self
- Sees self as Victimized/defensive
- Low expectations
- Finds it difficult to empathize with others

ANGER

EVIDENCES OF ANGER

1. Tension/stress release
2. Temper
3. Complaining
4. Bitterness
5. Control
6. Aggression/violence
7. Withdrawal/retreat
8. Non-relational

©atg/dcg

Determination Chart

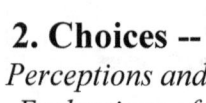

1. Beliefs—
What our experiences have taught us to believe about how life works

2. Choices --
Perceptions and Evaluations of How Life Works

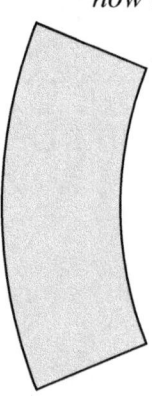
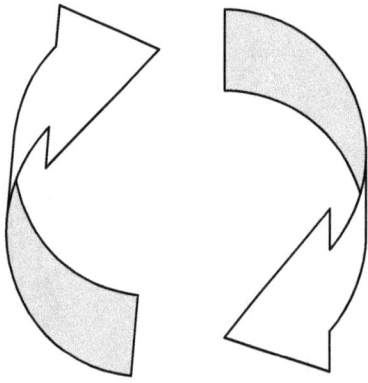
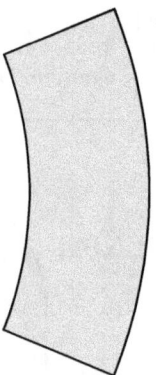

4. Actions –
What we do, moving upon what we assess to be actual and true.

3. Feelings –
What our inner being tells us is true for in regard to life direction

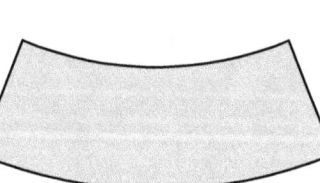

©atg/dcg

Session Three – Homework

1. Continue working on the list of your life experiences with authority figures, using your personal pictures to prod your memory.

   Make a list of the highlights in telling your story…. Don't use lots of detail unless you feel it will be helpful to get it out on paper. Sometimes, if you have a memory that brings pain to mind, it is good to remember the detail – that will help when we are walking through the healing process later.

   Note: Don't be concerned if painful memories do come to mind… It is usually the instances in our lives that have caused us the most pain that tend to surface – they give us clues as to where and when our emotional development slowed or stopped.

2. Please continue reading the first recommended book, and make notes on a separate piece of paper of areas where you relate to Mary Magdalene's story. If you have finished this book, please begin reading "The Divine Romance" by Gene Edwards.

3. Please memorize the scripture verse: Isaiah 41:10-13.

   "Do not fear, for I am with you; Do not anxiously look about you, for I am your God. I will strengthen you, surely I will help you, surely I will uphold you with My righteous right hand.' Behold, all those who are angered at you will be shamed and dishonored; Those who contend with you will be as nothing and will perish. "You will seek those who quarrel with you, but will not find them, Those who war with you will be as nothing and non-existent. "For I am the LORD your God, who upholds your right hand, Who says to you, 'Do not fear, I will help you.'

4. Please also take time to read Ephesians, chapters one and two each night this week, preferably at bedtime. .

Session Three ~
Personal Discovery Journal

Mentoring Assignment #3
Identifying the Attributes of God, Part 3

1. As we continue this journey toward whole-ness of soul, take a few moments to finish the second half of the journaling exercise from session one. To review, for some women, it is difficult to approach God at all, because He is presented as a male authority figure. Many of us deal with broken images of male authority, because earthly men have misrepresented Father in our lives. For some of us, the word "father" is a dirty word. For some, it calls to images of abuse and harshness. Whatever the response to the word, "father," each of us have areas where the correct understanding of male authority has been altered from the Creator's original plan. So, as we begin this process of healing, it is important that we gain an unfiltered grasp of just exactly Who we are dealing with, when we approach Father God.

In every life, there exists a filter, created by our perceptions and imprintings at an early age of development. In this ministry, we refer to this filter as the "father filter." By definition, it means, that every person on the planet filters their perception of their Heavenly Father, through their perception of their earthly father. And, subsequently, what we perceive to be normal as children, becomes the basis for how we approach life as adults.

Utilizing the following scriptures, please work through the final segment of our first step in discovering the attributes and nature of Father God provided for our understanding in the Word.

Scripture	Attribute

Isaiah 57:15 – "For thus says the High and Lofty One Who inhabits eternity, whose name *is* Holy: " I dwell in the high and holy *place, w*ith him *who* has a contrite and humble spirit, to revive the spirit of the humble, and to revive the heart of the contrite ones."

Hebrews 8:10-12

Psalm 119:11-12

Proverbs 14:12/ Proverbs 16:25 -- "There is a way *that seems* right to a man, but its end *is* the way of death."

Psalm 34:4-7

I John 5:14-15 – "Now this is the confidence that we have in Him, that if we ask anything according to His will, He hears us. And if we know that He hears us, whatever we ask, we know that we have the petitions that we have asked of Him."

Psalm 23

Scripture	**Attribute**

Galatians 4:4-7 – "But when the fullness of the time had come, God sent forth His Son, born of a woman, born under the law, to redeem those who were under the law, that we might receive the adoption as sons. And because you are sons, God has sent forth the Spirit of His Son into your hearts, crying out, "Abba, Father!" Therefore you are no longer a slave but a son, and if a son, then an heir of God through Christ."

Romans 8:15-16

Hebrews 4:16 – "Let us therefore come boldly to the throne of grace, that we may obtain mercy and find grace to help in time of need."

Matthew 18:1-4

Discoveries I made this week:

Please utilize these note pages as you listen to the recorded lecture for Session Four.

Ruth and Naomi – The Healing Journey
Session Four – Deceptions and Lies

I Timothy 2:14

How does deception happen?

Genesis 3:1-8

1. Eve listened to the lie.

    Romans 1:20-23

    She traded identity for it in her mind.
    (part of who Father had destined her to become)

2. She then chose to serve the lie
    Romans 6:14-18

    The lie became her source
    (she found a shortcut to being like God)

3. She deceived herself, believing the lie to be truth.

    II Corinthians 11:3-4

    The lie became her standard for behavior.

4. She ate the fruit – it became part of her being. She took it in. She shared it with those she loved. It brought change to him and all future generations..

    Colossians 2:6-8

    The lie tied her to the perception in every area of her life; inner & outer; physcal, emotional and spiritual It also bound her to the experience that brought the perception, stopping growth and change.

5. Rationalization then follows, because it normalizes our behavior rather than the Word of God.

    What is happening around us the standard for our beliefs, and our understanding of how life works. We compare ourselves and our experiences to other people's experiences, and we become passive and self-consumed.

© atg/dcg

What are the steps out?

1. Look at your life. Accept who you are, and where you are stuck.

2. Repent. Make a choice to turn around, pursuing change.

3. Ask the Holy Spirit to help you. Ask Him to open your eyes. Eph. 1:16-18

4. As He does open your eyes, He will show you the lies you have accepted as truth. He will also bring to mind the circumstances through which the perception was made.

5. When He does, don't deny it, don't argue with it. Face it. Remember that denial and cycling are what give pain its power.

6. Repent for buying into the lie.

7. Break the power the lie has had over your mind, but renouncing it. Tear down the stronghold, pleading the Blood and Name of Jesus Christ.

8. Forgive those who have wounded you, or who instigated the perception you bought into.

9. Apply the Word of God, which is truth; doing warfare in your mind against the thought processes and safety mechanisms you have allowed to tie you to oppression. It will take time, and repeated and intentional.

10. Find a safe friend you can share the struggles you are having with, and share mutually about what Father is doing in your life.

11. Don't expect your life in Jesus to go by the Big Bang Theory (event to event and experience to experience). Life in Jesus is a Day by Day Journey, and it takes time. II Corinthians 3:18

12. Continue to repeat this pattern for your development and healing, until you come to wholeness.

© atg/dcg

Lies That Tie Us To Oppression

The Lie: "God expects me to do things perfectly."

    The Truth: Galatians 3:3
                         II Cor. 12:9
                         Psalm 18:32

The Lie: "I need to keep a perfect environment."
The Truth: II Samuel 22:33

The Lie: "I must please everyone; I must keep everyone happy."
The Truth: Colossians 2:6-8

The Lie: "I need everyone's approval."
The Truth: Galatians 1:10

The Lie: "I need to be like everyone else in order to be right."
The Truth: II Corinthians 10:12

The Lie: "I must defend myself, or no one will.."
The Truth: Psalm 31:15
                         Psalm 91:1-3
                         Psalm 119:114

The Lie: "I must create a place for myself."
The Truth: Proverbs 18:16

The Lie: "Close relationships with other people are dangerous."
The Truth: Eccl. 4:9-12
                         Proverbs 27:9-10;
                         Proverbs 18:24

The Lie: "Being vulnerable is unsafe. I can't tell anyone my struggles."

    The Truth: James 5:16
                         Eph. 4:13-15

The Lie: "I am on the outside. I don't belong."

    The Truth: Ephesians 1:3-12

The Lie: "I must earn my place."

The Truth: *II Timothy 1:9*
                       Titus 3:5-7

The Lie: "What I do determines my worth."

The Truth: *Matt. 10:26-31*
                       Luke 12:6-7
                       Ephesians 2:8-10
                       Psalm 139:14-18

The Lie: "God does not want to talk to me."
The Truth: *John 16:12-15*

The Lie: "I must take the blame for there to be peace in my relationships."

The Truth: *Galatians 6:5*

The Lie: "Love and sexual expression are the same thing.."

The Truth: *I Thess. 4:3-8*
                       I Corinthians 13

The Lie: "Conflict is always bad."

The Truth: *Ephesians 6:12*

The Lie: "I can't trust anyone else with my heart, and my inner desires."

The Truth: *Ephesians 5:21*
                       I Cor. 13:4-7

The Lie: "I must make my own way."

The Truth: *I Peter 3:8-9*

The Lie: "Respect and fear are the same thing. I must fear authority."
The Truth: *II Timothy 1:7*
                       Romans 8:15-17

The Lie: "I must protect my own interests to be heard, and to be safe."
The Truth: *Philippians 2:3-4*
                       I Peter 4:8-11

The Lie: "I must be in control to be heard and to be safe."
The Truth: *Deut. 30:6*

The Lie: "When things go wrong, God doesn't accept me. There is something wrong with me."
    The Truth: Ephesians 2:4-7
                    Hebrews 4:14-16

The Lie: "It is too late for me to change. Too much has happened."
    The Truth: Hebrews 12:1-2

The Lie: "Anger is my empowerment to speak and be heard."
    The Truth: Eph. 4:26-27
                    James 1:19

The Lie: "Alcohol will make me feel better."
    The Truth: Proverbs 23:29-32

The Lie: "Pain is part of intimacy. Intimacy must be avoided for me to be safe."
    The Truth: John 15:4-8
                    Heb. 10:24-25

The Lie: "God likes other people more than He likes me."
    The Truth: Romans 2:11

The Lie: "I must make my own way.."

    The Truth: Psalm 138:7-8

The Lie: "My feelings determine truth for me."
    The Truth: Philippians 4:8

The Lie: "My perceptions and experiences determine truth."
    The Truth: Phil. 1:9-11
                    Psalm 51:6

The Lie: "When people don't agree with me, they don't love me."
    The Truth: Proverbs 11:3
                    Proverbs 17:9
                    Proverbs 27:6

The Lie: "God is mean, and I must earn His love."
    The Truth: Psalm 103:8-14

The Lie: "The bad things that happen in my life are in indication of God's will for me."

    The Truth: Jer. 29:11-13
                    II Samuel 22:3

The Lie: "I need to protect my own interests."
    The Truth: Psalm 5:11

The Lie: "When things are not going well for me, I do not have God's acceptance and approval."
    The Truth: James 1:2-4
    _____

The Lie: "God likes other people more than He likes me. He must have favorites."
    The Truth: Romans 2:11
    _____

The Lie: "It's too late for me to change."
    The Truth: Hebrews 12:1-2
    _____

The Lie: "Life can't be any better than this. I'm stuck."

    The Truth: Romans 8:28
                    Jer. 29:11-13

Four Legs of Personhood

- Voice
- Community
- Relationship
- Empowerment

Session Four – Homework

1. Please continue reading the first recommended reading book: "Journey" by Debbye Graafsma. As you read, make notes of the areas of pain where you identify with Mary Magdalene's experience in the book. If you have finished this book, another supplemental book of your choosing.

2. Please complete the worksheets for this session on the following pages.

3. Please memorize the scripture verse: Isaiah 54:17.

"No weapon that is formed against you will prosper; and every tongue that accuses you in judgment you will condemn. This is the heritage of the servants of the LORD, and their vindication is from Me," declares the LORD."

4. Please also take time to read Ephesians, chapters three and four this week each day, preferably at bedtime.

Session Four ~ Personal Discovery Journal

Mentoring Assignment #4
Discovering my relationship with Abba

1. Looking at the attributes you discovered in the homework for sessions one through three, take a few moments to consider each one. Which scriptures ministered to you most deeply? What were the attributes of Abba Father that appealed to you specifically from those scriptures?

2. Transfer those attributes to this page, making a bulleted list.

3. Many times, because of a lack of identity formation, we are unable to relate to God as Father, or even as Bridegroom. Sometimes, because of negative relationships and broken trust, we find ourselves unable to relate to God on the basis of a relationship. It becomes difficult for the heart to grasp the fullness of His never ending love and care for us. What representation of God can you relate to, in order to separate your understanding of His nature from those of other authority figures in your life to this point? Here are some suggestions.

He is:
- Our Father
- Our Bridegroom
- Our Shepherd
- Our Protector
- Our Rescuer
- Our King
- Our Master and Lord
- Our Advocate (he defends us to others)
- Our Vinedresser

He is:
- The light of the world
- The Standard
- The Boss
- Our Superhero
- Comforter
- Guide
- Friend
- Shelter
- Lover of your soul
- Keeper

Try to choose a representation of His nature, in order to experience a fresh and positive imprinting upon your inner life. Then, utilize the next page, and write out a description of this new understanding you have of just exactly Jesus is for you, in your life, right now. This description of Jesus needs to be a combination of all of the attributes that touch you most deeply – When you think about the nature of Jesus, what parts of His nature bring deep emotion? What causes hope to stir? These things need to be incorporated in your description. This description will become a tool in the growth process which you will come back to again and again.

<u>Note:</u> Transformation does not just happen in us – there is intentionality and hard work which attends it. This will probably be a difficult exercise, but it is the key that will determine how many doors of growth can be opened in your life later. So push through, plug in, and choose to move forward in your spiritual life.

My Description

Jesus is my _____

Imprinting description, cont'd

Imprinting description, cont'd

Discoveries I made this week:

Pease utilize these note pages as you listen to the recorded lecture for Session Five.

Ruth and Naomi – The Healing Journey
Session Five – All Knotted Up

My Description

Jesus is my _____

What keeps us from growing in our emotional lives?

The Truth About Ties that Binds us

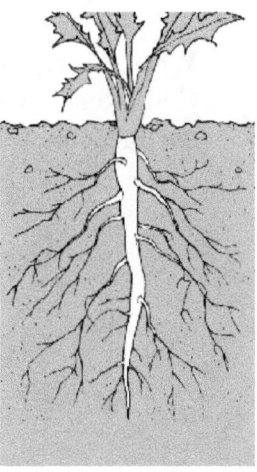

What Allows the Enemy Legal Access to our Lives

Here are some ways in which we can give the enemy access to our lives. In doing so, we lessen our ability to discern and follow-through with spiritual warfare.

- Immorality, outright sin, disobedience
- Holding an attitude of heart that disregards obedience
- Selfishness
- A critical spirit
- Evil speaking against other people, especially leadership and those in authority
- Not being aware of Satan's devices and characteristics
- Not knowing the Word of God and Father's purposes
- Not following through persistently in prayer and worship
- Allowing spiritual "single-eyed-ness and focus" to deteriorate
- Looking at the problem instead of the Lord Jesus
- Lost priorities in daily life
- Cursing others or situations
- Anger/violence/hatred
- Generational sin and infirmities
- Fatigue, weariness
- Doing instead of Being
- Inadequate Prayer Cover
- Not spending time with the Lord
- Becoming careless and passive
- Excusing or rationalizing sin

Many times, there can be an attack which is prolonged, and you feel that you are being faithful in the Word and in prayer. Be aware, also, in these times, that one of the devil's devices is to cause you to feel inadequate in prayer, so that you will stop praying.)

No one will ever be good enough in themselves. Our sufficiency is in Christ Jesus.

When this type of attack comes, the only solution is to run to the fortress of the Word of God. Renew your mind, by memorizing Scripture in regard to the areas of life where you are under attack.

Spiritual Strongholds

1. Generational Curses –   **(Exodus 20:5, Exodus 34:7, Deuteronomy 5:9)**

    Curses are an expected result of sins in these areas (see Deuteronomy 27 and 28) Idolatry, dishonesty, deception, dishonoring parents, cruelty to the helpless, sexual sins, disregard for the law.

To the degree that we obey the Father, allowing the Holy Spirit to renew our minds through His Word – to that degree, we can overcome Satan's efforts to ensnare us. (Matthew 16:22-23) Pray until you feel something shift in the spiritual realm. Don't give up if this battle becomes difficult.

2. Bondages --   (Galatians 5:1)
    a. **Unforgiveness** -- Compare the injustice you have suffered against your own injustice towards Father God. (See Matthew 6:14, and Ephesians 4:31-32)

        Renounce anger and resentment. Give up the desire to keep the wound Open in your heart by continually reliving the problem. Make a decision to forgive, since forgiveness begins in the will. Let go of all self-motivated desires, (self-pity, depression… etc.)

    b. **Grief and Self Pity** – Knowledge doesn't heal. Only the Blood of Jesus can heal and set free.

        Dealing with grief is a process. As you become aware of the source of your negative perspectives, give them over to the Holy Spirit, and allow Him to heal you. Give away your right to be right, and to hold on to the hurt and pain. He will settle the accounts. (See Proverbs 15:3, Proverbs 17:22, Isaiah 61:3)

    c. Addictions – Webster's definition "to devote or surrender oneself to something (or someone) obsessively"

        Addictions are: forms of spiritual idolatry
                               False barriers between the addict and God
                               Preventions of obedience to Father God
                               A demand for attention
                               A way for sin to perpetuate itself

        Addictions have a spiritual base. They are a direct reflection of a life of bondage and rebellion. They are sin, and must be repented for. An addiction is actually a misdirection of worship. Sometimes, it can have its root in seeds of emotional imprinting in a person's life.

d. **Rejection and Negative self-image** -- a person continually needs affirmation (more than is normal), and must have "self" fed, in order to feel accepted in any degree. Rejection has a spiritual base, usually in the past of the individual, and memories have formed a type of mold for the personality to follow. (See Proverbs 15:4, Proverbs 18:21)

Pray for a revelation knowledge of the Love of Father God to penetrate the wall of rejection. (See Romans 8:35-39, and Isaiah 54:17) Also, a more indepth ministry, such as "New Horizons," can equip the person for victorious Christian Life.

e. **Immoral Sexual Behavior** – An appetite for perversion
(See I Corinthians 6:16-18, Romans 6:23) Death comes in three forms – physical emotional and spiritual.

f. **Spirits of Death** – whether outwardly directed or inwardly directed. This is a murderous spirit towards others – suicidal when directed inward (See Psalm 118:17-19, and Isaiah 38:18-19)

g. **Occultic involvement** – Anything related to the occult (Deuteronomy 18 and 19) astrology, reading horoscopes, palm reading, Ouija boards, tarot cards, séances, fortune telling, witchcraft, divination, sorcery, magic, casting spells, casting hexes, voodoo, secret societies, etc.) Even if you don't take it seriously, evil spirits do.

Sometimes, a person can have something in their possession innocently, that is an abomination to the Lord, and not know it. Seek God into prayer, and ask the Lord to show you room by room what you need to "clean out" of your home. (Good examples: face masks from the West Indies or Africa, Greek mythological materials, American Indian tribal items, anything with deities from "other religions") See Deuteronomy 7:25

Session Five – Homework

1. Please continue reading your assigned reading book. Makes notes of what you are learning as you read. If possible, try to finish the book this week.

2. Using the photo journal of your life which you have developed so far, work through the workbook sheets on the following pages, regarding male authority figures.

3. Please complete the worksheets on the following pages. As you do so, complete the worksheets on the following pages, keep the description of Father God close by, and refer to it often, reminding yourself of His nature and character. Are there areas where you could make determination to choose to believe He is safe in His care for you? As you contemplate these things, journal your discoveries.

4. Please read the book of I John each night this week before you go to sleep. Before you close your eyes, ask the Holy Spirit to give you a deeper awareness of the God who is described in this chapter.

5. Please memorize Proverbs 31:25, 26 and 30:

   "Strength and dignity are her clothing, and she smiles at the future. She opens her mouth in wisdom, and the teaching of kindness is on her tongue. ... Charm is deceitful and beauty is vain, but a woman who fears the Lord, she shall be praised."

6. Please review all of your memorization verses this week, making sure they are rendered to your memory.

Hint: It is a good idea, when memorizing Scripture, to write verses out on index cards and carry them with you during the day, reviewing them when you have a moment or two. – When memorizing, read the verse out loud to yourself, several times each day, especially right before you go to sleep in the evening.

Session Five –
Personal Discovery Journal

Mentoring Assignment #5
Defining Male Authority Figures

1. Before any healing or recovery can take place within the life, there must be an established trust with the Healer. There must be a confidence above all else in the love and three-fold desired relationship –

    that Jesus desires to have with you as Savior and Healer,
    that the Holy Spirit desires to have with you as the Comforter,
    that the Father desires to have with you as Protector

2. There exists a problem of perceptions and life-filters, which have been placed within the life through imprinting and experiences: altering our true perceptions of the unlimited and unconditional love of God. The only way in which to receive a true understanding and perspective is to allow the Word of God to renew our mental understanding of the authority figure we have always understood to be God. When we do this, we come to a place of inner life, in which the perspective of Father God is separated from our conceptions of all other authority within our inner life.

3. And our understanding of Ultimate Authority, Father God, must be separated from any misunderstandings we currently hold regarding authority, before we can really relate to Him, to other people, or to ourselves, with any degree of health and wholeness.

4. With these three points in mind, look over the journal you have made of your life story to this point. Looking through the accounts, mark those memories related to male authority figures in your life. Then, please utilize the space provided here, to journal those particular memories and perceptions. Using the left hand column, please list those instances – and any additional memories that come to mind – it isn't important to keep them in sequence. You can also include instances with male authority figures in your life during the present time. Journal instances you remember that brought pain or a certain perception. If you need additional pages, just add them to this binder. It is best to be a thorough as you possibly can be in this process. If you have difficulty remembering a year or two, sometimes this type of journaling will help to stir the memories to the surface.

> As you journal, remember: Jesus understands our weaknesses, and knows exactly how we feel. He was rejected too.   (See Hebrews 4:15/ Isaiah 53:3)

As you journal, remember: Jesus was mocked and beaten; and was falsely accused. (See Luke 22:63-64, Mark 14:57-58 and Luke 23:1-25)

As you journal, remember: Jesus was conceived before His mother was married. He was separated from His real Father, and lived with His earthly father. (See Matthew 1:18 and 23/ Matthew 1:19-25

Now, perhaps with a prayer partner, go back through the experiences you have listed, and, utilizing the right hand column, write down the perceptions and determinations you made about how life works. These determinations and perceptions are also called "inner judgments," or "life perceptions." For example: because a girl was violated against her will, she might make an inner decision that all men are out to hurt her, so she subconsciously decides to hate or distrust all men in general. Try to pull from the experiences and feelings you have listed, what the imprinting choices were which you made – whether conscious or subconscious at the time, in regard to your relationship with male authority figures.

Is there a current thread that you see beginning to unfold in these experiences? What is it?

_____

_____

_____

_____

What role models were provided for you of adult life?

_____

_____

_____

_____

What example did you admire?

_____

_____

_____

What role did you find yourself hating?

_____

_____

_____

In what ways have you tried to deny these points of imprinting in your life?

_____

_____

_____

Spend time with a prayer partner, making confession for the choices you have made in your life to this point based upon these perceptions. Ask them to agree with you, in cutting off these thought patterns, and mindsets from influencing your life. Repent for withdrawal and inner retreat, and ask the Holy Spirit to heal your will, and enable you to release these offenses.

Make the choice to grow past these inner decisions. Repent for believing the lies that led you to these places where you have become "stuck." It is okay to feel the hurt from those experiences. When you do, allow your heart to grieve, and share what is happening inside of you with your prayer partner. It is a good idea at this point to surrender to the Holy Spirit your personal right to be wounded, because holding on to the wound has become part of your present identity. Let go of the inner demand to get even, or even receive an apology. Release the settling of accounts to the hands of Jesus.

If the pain is deep, it might take a little while to do these things. We are headed toward the ability to really forgive and let go of the past. Remember, forgiveness is a decision, not a process. However, coming to healing and release is a process, and life journey. Your emotions will eventually come into agreement with your confession. It just takes time. Allow yourself to take that time. Father isn't pushing you, or demanding from you. He loves you, and wants to see healing happen on a deep level, not just in surface actions.

When you have walked through these things, take some time with your prayer partner, and make some healthy confessions for your own growth. Break off generational ties, soul ties, and attachments, which have fed those perceptions in your life, causing you to become stuck in this place of development. When you do, the Holy Spirit takes you at your word, and He goes to work immediately.

Give thanks to the Lord for His grace that cleanses us and makes us free from the past. Ask Him to develop your heart to respond with capacity for His Presence, and with health.

Please utilize these note pages as you listen to the recorded lecture for Session Six.

Ruth and Naomi – The Healing Journey
Session Six – Truth & the Problem of Denial

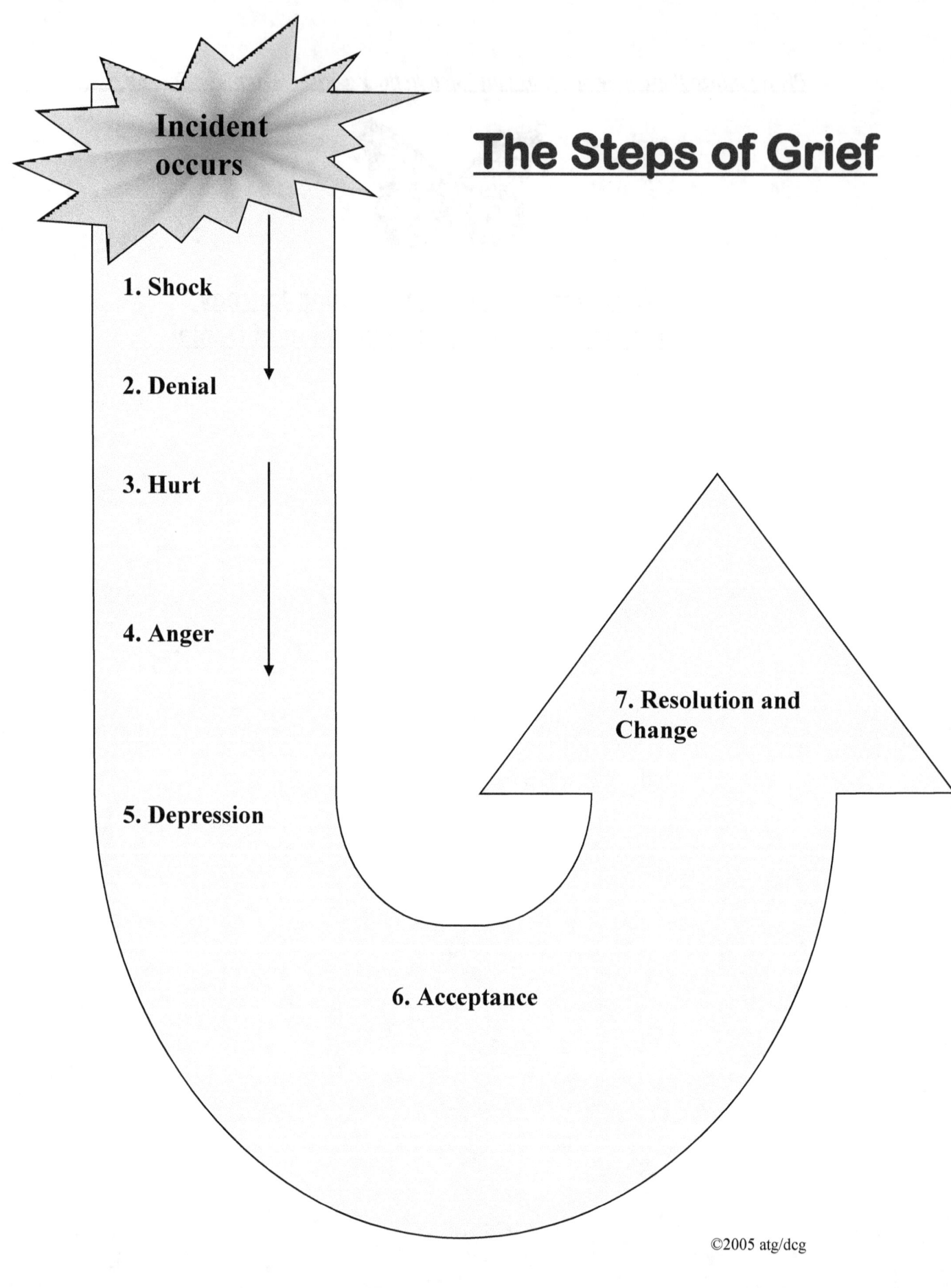

The Steps of Grief
Denial focus

Incident occurs

1. Shock

2. Denial

1. blaming
2. placing all fault
3. protesting (justice)
4. control (I'll fix it)
5. bargaining (mental or action)
6. compensating (approval mechanism)
7. minimalizing
8. rationalizing
9. "spiritualizing" – gloss
10. fragmentation
11. withdrawal/retreat
12. addictions
13. coping
14. self-defense
15. Religiosity
16. Escalated outbursts of Rage

3. Hurt

1. victim's mentality
2. hyper-sensitivity
3. defensiveness
4. low expectations

4. Anger

5. Depression – one form is _____ turned _____

©2005, atg/dcg

Determination Chart

1. Beliefs—
What we believe about how life works as it relates to our own lives.

2. Choices --
Perceptions and Evaluations of How Life Works

4. Actions –
What we do, moving upon what we assess to be actual and true.

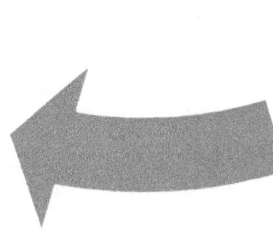

3. Feelings –
What our inner being tells us is true for in regard to life direction

©,atg/dcg

What is truth?

Psalm 51:6   hidden place – Hebrew word: *catham,*

                       (meaning= stopped up, sealed and secret)

I Timothy 1:4-5

I Samuel 28:6

Joel 2:28

Deuteronomy 13:1

How To Expose & Break the Power of Fear

*"For God has not given us
a spirit of fear, but of power,
and of love, and of a sound mind."
II Timothy 1:7*

1. A situation occurs, sometimes traumatic, which opens a door for fear and torment within the soul. The circumstance is either re-lived, or is repressed, depending upon the person's ability to deal with it at the given time.

2. The wound remains open within the soul, and continually influences choices made in various life-areas. Eventually, it sends out "runners" within the soul that are evidenced as forms of fear.

3. Rather than deal with each attribute of fear, it is better to go after the memory, which is the legal ground the enemy has gained to torment the person.

4. Ask the Holy Spirit to reveal the circumstance. Repent for opening the door to the spirit of Fear, and for giving it place, by accommodating it. Renounce its legal hold. Cut off generational ties to fear within the family, which have served to make it stronger, and have reinforced its influence and ability to rule the life. Forgive those who were involved in exposing the person to Fear. Release the right to hold on the attributes of fear as part of the personality. Apply the Blood of Jesus Christ. Anoint with oil, and break the yoke of bondage.

How Fear Takes Hold

"For God has not given us a spirit of fear, but of power, and of love, and of a sound mind."
II Timothy 1:7

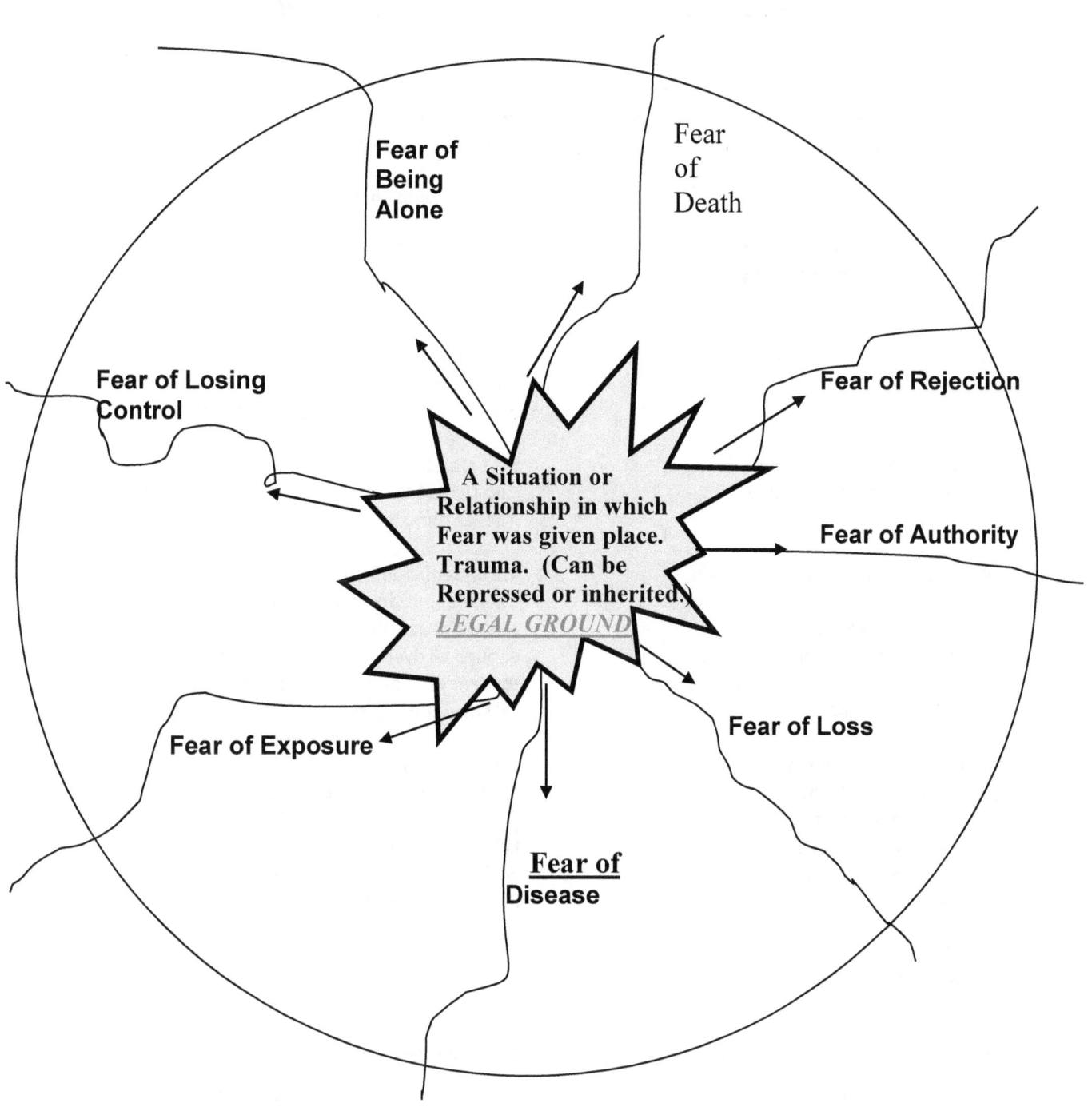

The Difference between Conviction and Condemnation

Conviction

(The work of the Holy Spirit, creating healthy Development and growth – invokes a desire to Follow and learn)

(creates right relationship)

1. Causes a person to flee into the Presence of God. "Running to see Dad and talk things out."

2. Aids in walking with God. Knowledge of being justified.

3. Failure and sin are removed, to greatly help fellowship with the Father.

4. Although conviction can cause you to feel miserable until you pray and repent, it is very specific in its dealing.—a specific instance requires a specific response. Conviction contains NO REJECTION.

Psalm 139:23-24. It is the Holy Spirit's job to search your heart. You cannot search and deal with all of your life's issues alone, and then present what you have found to Father God.

Jeremiah 17:10
II Corinthians 5:17

CLEANSING!!

End result = *PEACE*

I John 1:9

Condemnation

(The work of Hell's minions, creating an umbrella of rejection, disapproval and religious judgment.)

sees problems (drives away)

1. Hinders approach to God. Afraid of His responses.

2. Hinders fellowship with God. "He doesn't want to spend time with me, I'm not good enough."

3. Looks at failures as grounds for having no rights to God's fellowship. However, it never removes those failures.

4. Condemnation comes as an over-all general put-down. A person doesn't feel a sense of approval; just "bad," and not enough all over. Condemnation invokes a tendency to compare yourself with others and always come up short.

Romans 8:1-2. Christ does not operate in condemnation, but in the law of the Spirit of Life.
Ephesians 1 – He wants us to walk in understanding of His Plan and destiny for each of our lives.

BURDENING!!

End result = *GUILT/SHAME*

Psalm 32:3

© ATG/dcg

HOW TO TELL WHAT VOICE YOU ARE HEARING

There are three sources of direction given to us in the Word of God. Be careful to discern through pray which voice it is you are hearing.

1. **The Voice of Father God speaking through the Holy Spirit.** If it is His voice, it will always agree with the Word – and not just one verse, but several verses, or a theme of scripture, within its context. (It will never take one verse out of context to prove a point – that creates confusion.)

2. **Your own inner voice**, bringing up a thought, based on your own logic, intellect, and self-centered emotions.

3. **A demonic voice**. The fruit of this voice is torment, fear, condemnation and strife.

What to do if you are confused as to what voice you are hearing.

1. *Repent for opening any door to the enemy.*

2. *Apply the Blood of Jesus to your emotions and thought life.*

3. *Bind every voice that is not the voice of the Holy Spirit.*

4. *Ask the Lord to speak to you again.*

5. *Wait for more direction. Never act quickly when you are unsure.*

6. *Seek the heart of the Father. Trust Him to lead you.*

A Child's Core Needs

These core yearnings/needs must be met during cognitive (physical) development, for a person to have a healthy life-view, and a complete sense of Personhood.

1. A safe secure environment.

2. A constant reinforcement of personal worth

3. Repeated messages that the person is valued, unique, & special

4. Unconditional Love & acceptance

5. Basic Care & nurturing

6. Encouragement to Grow – develop personal gifts & talents.

7. A pathway to fellowship with God

8. Connection & belonging

9. Feeling needed & Useful

10. Inner emotional & character building for destiny fulfillment

©,atg/dcg

Session Six – Homework

1. Please continue reading your assigned reading book. Makes notes of what you are learning as you read. If possible, try to finish the book this week.

2. Using the photo journal of your life which you have developed so far, work through the workbook sheets on the following pages, regarding female authority figures. If you become overwhelmed, call a friend you trust to pray with you. Allow your heart to become encouraged in the love of God.

3. Please complete the worksheets on the following pages. As you do so, complete the worksheets on the following pages, keep the description of Father God close by, and refer to it often, reminding yourself of His nature and character. Are there areas where you could make determination to choose to believe He is safe in His care for you? As you contemplate these things, journal your discoveries.

4. Please read the book of I John each night this week before you go to sleep. Before you close your eyes, ask the Holy Spirit to give you a deeper awareness of the God who is described in this chapter.

5. Please memorize Proverbs 31:25, 26 and 30:

    "Strength and dignity are her clothing, and she smiles at the future. She opens her mouth in wisdom, and the teaching of kindness is on her tongue. ... Charm is deceitful and beauty is vain, but a woman who fears the Lord, she shall be praised."

6. Please review all of your memorization verses this week, making sure they are rendered to your memory.

Hint: It is a good idea, when memorizing Scripture, to write verses out on index cards and carry them with you during the day, reviewing them when you have a moment or two. – When memorizing, read the verse out loud to yourself, several times each day, especially right before you go to sleep in the evening.

Session Six ~
Personal Discovery Journal

Mentoring Assignment #6
The Power of Female Authority Figures

    As women, we are designed to be more emotional and sensitive than men are. As little girls, we not only are affected by the treatment and relationship we share with those male authority figures in our lives, but also we receive training from those role models and mentors in our lives, also known as female authority figures. From the women in our lives, we have learned how to process pain, how to grieve, how to respond to conflict, and how to survive on a daily basis. We have learned to view life experiences either negatively or as a challenge, producing positive growth. We have learned how to relate to other women, how to respond to male authority, how to view children, and how to view ourselves. The role of female authority is very powerful in our lives.

    And sadly, even if we have had a positive view of male authority, it is possible to have processed negatively in our lives, due to the fact that it is the mother who interprets the father's motives and actions, especially if that father is non-communicative, or unaffectionate. With this in mind, please take a moment to review the beginning instructions from assignment number one. Now, with those points of ministry in mind, please utilize the space provided here, to journal memories and perceptions you currently have regarding **female** authority. Using the left hand column, please list and refer to all female authority figures – present and past. Journal instances you remember that brought pain or a certain perception, as well as the result of the experience in your life. Usually, our difficulties as women with female authority sadly have to do with feeling dominated or controlled. Perhaps there was a lack of mother/daughter bonding in your life, and you have never learned to relate to other women as safe and healthy friends. Journal those instances here.

As you journal, remember: Jesus understands our weaknesses, and knows exactly how we feel. He was not received well by His earthly family. (See Hebrews 4:15/ John 7:1-5)

As you journal, remember: Jesus was kept up all night by his accusers. He was spat upon and struck.. He was hated for no reason. (See Luke 24:45-53/ Matthew 26:67/ John 15:24-25

As you journal, remember: Jesus was abandoned by His real Father, so that forever afterwards the Father could look through Jesus' eyes to see you in your time of need. (See Matthew 27:45-46, and Mark 15:33-34)

Now, perhaps with a prayer partner, go back through the experiences you have listed, and, utilizing the right hand column, see if you can tell where some of the thought patterns about how life works have come from – sometimes we call them "inner judgments," or "life perceptions." For example: because a girl was violated against her will, she might make an inner decision that all women are out to hurt her, so she subconsciously decides to hate or distrust all women in general. Try to pull from the experiences and feelings you have listed, what the imprinting choices were which you made – whether conscious or subconscious at the time, in regard to your relationship with female authority figures.

Is there a current thread that you see beginning to unfold in these experiences? What is it?

_____

_____

_____

What role models were provided for you of adult life?

_____

_____

_____

What example did you admire?

_____

_____

_____

What role did you find yourself hating?

___

In what ways have you tried to deny these points of imprinting in your life?

___

Spend time with a prayer partner, making confession for the choices you have made in your life to this point based upon these perceptions. Ask them to agree with you, in cutting off these thought patterns, and mindsets from influencing your life. Repent for withdrawal and inner retreat, and ask the Holy Spirit to heal your will, and enable you to release these offenses.

Make the choice to grow past these inner decisions. Repent for believing the lies that led you to these places where you have become "stuck." It is okay to feel the hurt from those experiences. When you do, allow your heart to grieve, and share what is happening inside of you with your prayer partner. It is a good idea at this point to surrender to the Holy Spirit your personal right to be wounded, because holding on to the wound has become part of your present identity. Let go of the inner demand to get even, or even receive an apology. Release the settling of accounts to the hands of Jesus.

If the pain is deep, it might take a little while to do these things. We are headed toward the ability to really forgive and let go of the past. Remember, forgiveness is a decision, not a process. However, coming to healing and release is a process, and life journey. Your emotions will eventually come into agreement with your confession. It just takes time. Allow yourself to take that time. Father isn't pushing you, or demanding from you. He loves you, and wants to see healing happen on a deep level, not just in surface actions.

When you have walked through these things, take some time with your prayer partner, and make some healthy confessions for your own growth. Break off generational ties, soul ties, and attachments, which have fed those perceptions in your life, causing you to become stuck in this place of development. When you do, the Holy Spirit takes you at your word, and He goes to work immediately.

Give thanks to the Lord for His grace that cleanses us and makes us free from the past. Ask Him to develop your heart to respond with capacity for His Presence, and with health.

Please utilize these note pages as you listen to the recorded lecture for Session Seven.

Ruth and Naomi – The Healing Journey
Session Seven – How Shame Becomes a Template for Living

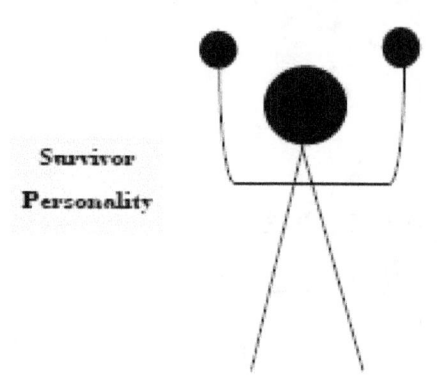

Survivor Personality

Survivor Characteristics
- Emotional "power"
- Decision making
- Limited feeling & expression
- Demanding
- Must be heard
- Exerts control
- Conditional approval
- Guarded by: anger/withdrawal
- Stern/strict/can be abusive
- Rules/justice based
- Center of orbit/anger

In order for healthy living to occur, the false empowerment within the survivor personality must be dismantled. For this to happen properly, the Wall of Self-Protection must be exchanged for appropriate and healthy boundaries in relationships.

Wall of Self-Protection. Constructed of Fear and/or Pride (Fear + Pride = Control)

IQ
EQ

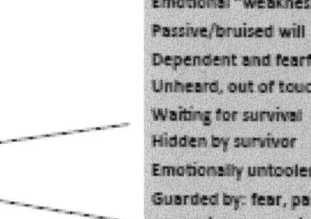

Automatic Self-Protective Defense Mechanisms

Elements of Denial manifest as a choice to adjust to the environment with an IQ or EQ personality style

Hidden/Vulnerable Personality

Vulnerable Characteristics
- Emotional "weakness"
- Passive/bruised will
- Dependent and fearful
- Unheard, out of touch
- Waiting for survival
- Hidden by survivor
- Emotionally untooled
- Guarded by: fear, pain, complaint, depression, bitterness, anger

In order for healthy living to occur, the hidden core personality of the inner child, must be validated and given voice to communicate emotions and perceptions. This most vulnerable personality must then be strengthened to stand to take its place in life management and decision-making.

Personal Application

©dg/atg

How Do We Learn to Nurture Shame?

Models of Authority	Actions	Message the Child Receives
1. Unprepared parents	1. Does not know what childhood should look like. 2. Image based; worried about what people think. 3. Expect child to be a small adult 4. Unreasonable expectations; perfectionism 5. Expects the child to already know 6. "You should know better" 7. "What's wrong with you?" 8. "Where did you learn to act like that?"	1. I can't measure up 2. I have to figure things out alone 3. I'll never be good enough 4. There's something wrong with me that I can't fix.
2. Unavailable parents	1. Emotionally distant; no heart connection 2. Pre-occupied with work, activities, addiction 3. Child is drawn into the orbit around parents 4. Too busy for play; disinterested 5. Doesn't attend child's events 6. No celebration of effort 7. Work oriented achievement/Performance 8. Always time crunched; no quantity time	1. My needs don't matter 2. Others are more important than me 3. I'm not important enough 4. There's no one for me 5. I'm in the way 6. I have less worth than others
3. Unloving parents	1. Abuse – knowingly, or unknowingly 2. Hands off – verbal, emotional, financial – intimidation, withdrawal, control 3. Hands on – physical, sexual	1. I shouldn't be here 2. I don't belong – I'm outside 3. I'm not wanted 4. I'm not worth it – I have no value 5. There's something wrong with me I can't fix.

0-5 years

Magical Thinking = "I caused the events in my world; happily ever after; everyone needs to be happy"

Self-Concept = The way I fit into the world (learned in pre-cognitive years); from cues and signals received by those in relationship. What works for my survival

Models and Imprintings for adult life

"I will become the one who has hurt me the most, because I am bound to my pain. My focus becomes my blockage to growth."

Messages of "Toxic Shame" or "False Guilt"

"There is something wrong with me that makes me worth-less than others."

Convictional Sorrow

In Relationships With others

Strengthens us

To say "I was wrong, I'm sorry, please forgive me," when we have caused injury to others.

Helps us to establish personal boundaries as to our own privacy, modesty and trust levels

Shows us when we are "over the line," and serves as our conscience

In Spiritual Understanding

Draws Us

Into relationship with Abba Father

Shows us our sin, and encourages repentance (change)

Encourages us to desire to grow and pursue relationship with those who will mentor us in Spiritual Life.

Keeps us tuned to the Holy Spirit

Toxic Shame

In Relationships With others

Isolates Us

Deceives us to pursue perfectionism (counterfeit for grace)

Develops codependency in us

Tell us we can never be good enough to earn approval

Teaches us to deny our feelings and grief

In Spiritual Understanding

Weakens Us

Creates an inner fortress of pride and self-sufficiency

Tells us we are distant from God, and brings condemnation

We try to earn our place, and earn God's love

Brings confusion

Family Diagrams

*Note: Father God's plan and purpose for family life is a safe and secure place; emotionally, physically, and spiritually for each family member. Family Life is a God-created environment where Design and Destiny can be discovered, encouraged, developed and pursued with purpose. While Marriage is a Place **where intimate relationship is developed** between a man and woman who have chosen each other for a life partnership, Family Life is a place **where the children are to be developed** and allowed to grow, encouraged by the parents.*

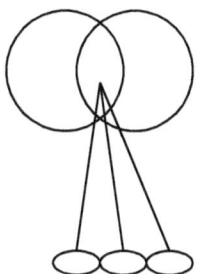

Healthy Family
Father and Mother have learned to operate together, and present decisions and options to children together, as a unified team. Children are ministered to on an equal basis, with no favoritism shown or expressed. **Focus: Abba's plan for the common good.**

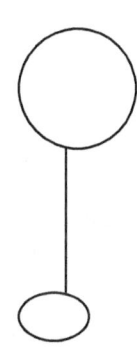

Healthy Single Parent Relationship
Each parent has learned to connect with the child's inner person, and can communicate from a relational point of view future goals and discipline. **Focus: Abba's plan for the common good.**

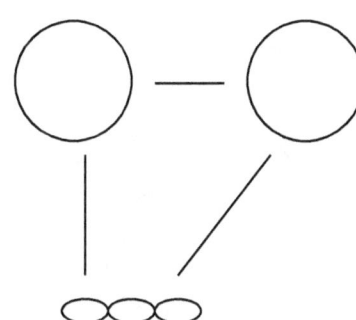

Unhealthy Parent Relationships
Parents are unconnected with each other and with the children. Communication takes place regarding task and fact levels only. Children receive communication, but there is no connection. Result: children receive a sense of abandonment and isolation, and become task oriented for approval. There is little or no affection communicated. **Focus: Personal rights, needs and/or appetites.**

© 2006

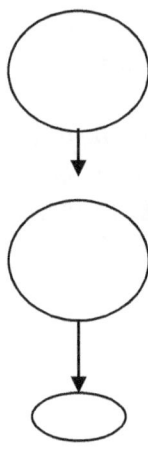

Authority Driven Model (unhealthy)

One parent is seen as having all authority, and communicates with the children through a chain-of-command, without personal relationship with the child. The child is distanced in the relationship and has no opportunity to appeal or question decisions. Voice and Identity are diminished within the family, for all members except the family member with the most authority.

Also within this model, one parent must continually explain the other to the child. The parent in the explaining role tends to lose personal identity and become co-dependent, seeking to keep peace in the home at any price. Acceptance is performance oriented. **Focus: To succeed on all fronts. To meet expectations**

The Abuse Model

The parents have experienced relational failure in their own abilities to build a marriage. They are emotionally distanced. Communication regarding the relationship is made to the child, and the child feels they must choose between parents.

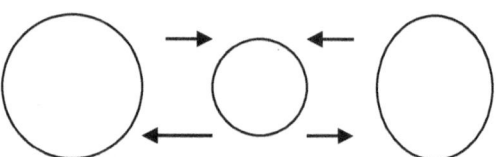

The child becomes the caretaker, and must meet the emotional needs of the parent; many times this involves verbal, emotional, physical, or sexual abuse (order of progression). The child must continually choose between parents, and perceives they must keep everyone happy. Identity development is stopped, and the child must choose an alternate "power" personality to survive. If a "power" personality is not found, the child will become depressed and lethargic. Approval is shame based

Focus: To survive

The Island Model

The parents have experienced relational failure in their own abilities to build a marriage. They are emotionally distanced. There is no communication.

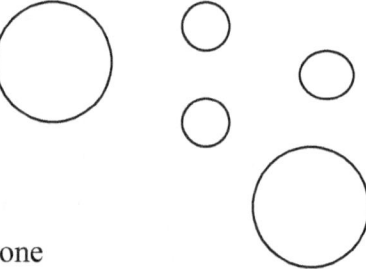

Everyone in the family lives in a separate environment. Everyone
Is taking care of themselves, and no one is connected emotionally. There
Is no care on mutual level. There are no bonding moments that can be remembered in this model
Focus: To survive

© 2006 dcg/atg

Session Seven – Homework

1. Please read the second required reading book in your supplementary reading list. .

2. If new memories come to mind regarding authority figures, add them to the journal entries you completed during the last few sessions. Looking at your life story journal, take a few moments to think about the role of female authority figures in your life, and journal any memories that come to mind into your life story sheets.

3. Please memorize the scripture verse: Psalm 103: 8 -- "The Lord is gracious, full of compassion, slow to anger, and great in mercy." Please also read Ephesians, chapter five and six this week.

4. Please complete the worksheets on the following pages.

Session Seven –
Personal Discovery Journal
Mentoring Assignment #7
Taking Hold of the Promises, Part A

1. Please take a moment to look over the past three assignments we have completed together.

    The first step in the Ruth and Naomi assignments was to help you to find a representation of Jesus, and of Father God, that could be separated from the filters dealing with authority relationships presently within your life. Father God is unlike any father on earth, and Jesus is His representation. Many times, due to bruising within the soul, women find themselves unable to respond to God, when He is represented as "Father," or "Bridegroom," or even "Brother," since those earthly relationships have held such pain –

    The second step was to help you to put into writing all of the emotions and perceptions you have learned to use in coping with life, as circumstances and relationships have presented themselves to you. We then asked you to assign each emotion to a male figure who was or has been present in your life experience, in order to help you to grasp the touch-points in your life, where those male authority figures became part of your identity formation. – and even those situations in which your perceptions and inner reactions brought about the beginnings of safety mechanisms, survival-ism, or control.

If you have not fulfilled the first two steps completely, please understand that it is absolutely necessary for you to have a representation of the Person of Jesus, who is real and almost tangible within your heart – this is the foundation stone upon which the rest of the mentoring steps are built. Please be sure that you have a graspable, understandable, scriptural representation with whom you sense a heart connect on a deep level.

2. We will take time during our Group Session for you to pray with a prayer partner, and go over the representation of the Person of Jesus, that you feel the Lord has provided for you, based upon the Scripture. Share your description of this representation with her, and ask for her input, in order to insure that you are being scripturally sound, as well as experientially open. This will help to deepen the picture you already are sensing.

3. Now we come to the subject of trust. It is absolutely essential in our spiritual and emotional growth as believers that we develop the ability to be transparent, honest, open and trusting not only of the Holy Spirit, but also of each other within the body of Christ. The choice to become a risk-taker, who places trust outside of oneself requires a great deal of courage and must be driven by a desire to grow into spiritual maturing more than anything else in life.

Are you willing to begin the journey to trust the Lord Jesus completely with your heart, and let Him bring you to full maturity? _____

Write out a prayer of commitment here.

_____

_____

_____

_____

_____

_____

4. When we begin to trust, it is important that we realize that before we are able to trust any other person, we must first become able to fully trust Jesus to take care of us. Please utilize the following scriptures. After looking up the scripture in the left hand column, please give a description of the trustworthiness of Jesus in the right hand column.

Scripture	Description
Genesis 21:1 *"And the LORD visited Sarah as He had said, and the LORD did for Sarah as He had spoken"*.	
Genesis 28:15	
Deuteronomy 4:31 *"(for the LORD your God is a merciful God), He will not forsake you nor destroy you, nor forget the covenant of your fathers which He swore to them.*	
Deuteronomy 7:8-9	
Deuteronomy 31:6 *"Be strong and of good courage, do not fear nor be afraid of them; for the LORD your God, He is the One who goes with you. He will not leave you nor forsake you."*	
Joshua 21:45	
I Samuel 12:22 *"For the LORD will not forsake His people, for His great name's sake, because it has pleased the LORD to make you His people."*	

| Scripture | Description |
|---|---|//

II Samuel 22:31 *"As for God, His way is perfect; The word of the LORD is proven; He is a shield to all who trust in Him."*

Psalm 5:11

Psalm 9:10 *"And those who know Your name will put their trust in You; For You, LORD, have not forsaken those who seek You."*

Psalm 32:10

Psalm 33:4 *"For the word of the LORD is right, and all His work is done in truth."*

Psalm 33:18

Psalm 34:2-8 *"My soul shall make its boast in the LORD; The humble shall hear of it and be glad. Oh, magnify the LORD with me, and let us exalt His name together. I sought the LORD, and He heard me, and delivered me from all my fears. They looked to Him and were radiant, and their faces were not ashamed. This poor man cried out, and the LORD heard him, and saved him out of all his troubles. The angel of the LORD encamps all around those who fear Him, And delivers them. Oh, taste and see that the LORD is good; Blessed is the man who trusts in Him!*

Psalm 34:22

Scripture	Description
Psalm 36:7 *"How precious is Your lovingkindness, O God! Therefore the children of men put their trust under the shadow of Your wings."*	
Psalm 37:28	
Psalm 40:4 *"Blessed is that man who makes the LORD his trust, and does not respect the proud, nor such as turn aside to lies."*	
Psalm 84:5	
Psalm 89:8 *"O LORD God of hosts, Who is mighty like You, O LORD? Your faithfulness also surrounds You."*	
Psalm 111:5-9	
Psalm 94:14	

Scripture	Description
Psalm 91 *"He who dwells in the secret place of the Most High shall abide under the shadow of the Almighty. I will say of the LORD, "He is my refuge and my fortress; My God, in Him I will trust." Surely He shall deliver you from the snare of the fowler and from the perilous pestilence. He shall cover you with His feathers, and under His wings you shall take refuge; His truth shall be your shield and buckler. You shall not be afraid of the terror by night, nor of the arrow that flies by day, Nor of the pestilence that walks in darkness, Nor of the destruction that lays waste at noonday. A thousand may fall at your side, and ten thousand at your right hand; But it shall not come near you. Only with your eyes shall you look, And see the reward of the wicked. Because you have made the LORD, who is my refuge, Even the Most High, your dwelling place, No evil shall befall you, Nor shall any plague come near your dwelling; For He shall give His angels charge over you, To keep you in all your ways. In their hands they shall bear you up, lest you dash your foot against a stone. You shall tread upon the lion and the cobra, the young lion and the serpent you shall trample underfoot. "Because he has set his love upon Me, therefore I will deliver him; I will set him on high, because he has known My name. He shall call upon Me, and I will answer him; I will be with him in trouble; I will deliver him and honor him. With long life I will satisfy him, and show him My salvation."*	
Psalm 118:8-9	
Psalm 119:89	

Looking back over the explanations of Abba Father's promises you have kept track of in this journaling assignment, make a short list here of the promises that ministered comfort to you – what elements of these promises to you from the Word present you with a different understanding of our God's nature?

Please utilize these note pages as you listen to the recorded lecture for Session Eight.

**Ruth and Naomi – The Healing Journey
Session Eight – The Composition of a Princess**

The Composition of a Princess

She has it all together

She keeps up appearances

She can spot a phony

She has enough experience to tell you the answer

She doesn't have time to be weak

She can run the house alone

She knows how the kids should be raised

Her husband just doesn't get it sometimes

She wants to be loved

She needs to be understood

She's screaming, but no one can hear her

She feels numb

© ATG/dcg

The Princess' Castle

1. Trigger Point =
Loaded and Volatile Destructive.
Paybacks FEAR

2. Control – Unsurrendered Pain – Insecurity hidden. Lack of trust. "Can take care of herself." Suspicious of men. **REJECTION**

3. Resistance/ Stubbornly Willful Survivor. Inability to receive love. Waits for personal terms to be met before she responds. Silently sets terms. Defensive. Distrusts men. **PRIDE/ INDEPENDENCE**

JEZEBEL STEPS IN TO INFLUENCE

JEZEBEL TAKES THE THRONE

JEZEBEL RULES

4. Manipulation – May or may not be sexual. Sets terms for acceptance and direction of relationships. The more intimate the relationship, the more terms. Pouts, uses threats and weapons to get desired result. Rejects what she cannot control. Suspicious of God/ Holds her own agenda. **ANGER/REVENGE**

5. Witchcraft – Deposes and/or challenges the man of God/ sets up own throne—destroys spiritual authority. Despises and cannot apply the Word of the Lord – will not receive correction, rather accuses those giving it. Must be source. Must be heard. Unteachable. Unwilling to yield. Sexual manipulation for gratification. REBELLION

© ATG/dcg

The Princess and Her Man

1. She discounts the value of her husband's words and desires. Her own thoughts on issues which pertain to their relationship are more important than his.

2. She inwardly disdains and can be disgusted with male leadership. She finds herself thinking, "A woman could do this job better." She also finds herself, at odds with women in leadership who defer to the male authority figure. She has very little difficulty disregarding instruction.

3. She blames her husband's mistakes for any difficulty she or the family might find themselves in. She wants to be assessed according to her intentions, but requires a higher standard for her husband. When her husband needs counsel or waits to handle an area, she is more than ready to take control of it.

4. She feels she is the only one who should handle the household monies, and make decisions about meeting the family's needs.

5. She makes veiled accusations against those in authority (usually sexual or promiscuous in nature), whether because of apparitions or suspicions within her own mind. This stops her from trusting her broken areas in these areas for counsel and healing.

6. She uses persuasion and concerted opinion to see that things go her way. She can be very manipulative, and not recognize it as a spirit of control.

7. She speaks down to her husband, and other male authority figures. She challenges choices and direction chosen by those men. Will not release trust to those in authority, unless she is allowed to retain control to a great degree.

© ATG/dcg

Spiritual Strongholds

1. **Generational Curses –** **(Exodus 20:5, Exodus 34:7, Deuteronomy 5:9)**

    Curses are expected results when a person sins in these areas
    (see Deuteronomy 27 and 28)
    Idolatry, dishonesty, deception, dishonoring parents, cruelty to the
    helpless, sexual sins, disregard for the law.

To the degree that we obey the Father, allowing the Holy Spirit to renew our minds through His Word – to that degree, we can overcome Satan's efforts to ensnare us. (Matthew 16:22-23) Pray until you feel something shift in the spiritual realm. Don't give up if this battle becomes difficult.

2. **Bondages --** (Galatians 5:1)
    h. **Unforgiveness --** Compare the injustice you have suffered against your own injustice towards Father God. (See Matthew 6:14, and Ephesians 4:31-32)

    Renounce anger and resentment. Give up the desire to keep the wound
    Open in your heart by continually reliving the problem. Make a decision to forgive, since forgiveness begins in the will. Let go of all self-motivated desires, (self-pity, depression… etc.)

    i. **Grief and Self Pity –** Knowledge doesn't heal. Only the Blood of Jesus can heal and set free.

    Dealing with grief is a process. As you become aware of the source of your negative perspectives, give them over to the Holy Spirit, and allow Him to heal you. Give away your right to be right, and to hold on to the hurt and pain. He will settle the accounts. (See Proverbs 15:3, Proverbs 17:22, Isaiah 61:3)

    j. **Addictions –** Webster's definition "to devote or surrender oneself to something (or some*one*) obsessively"

    Addictions are: forms of spiritual idolatry
    False barriers between the addict and God
    Preventions of obedience to Father God
    A demand for attention
    A way for sin to perpetuate itself

Addictions have a spiritual base. They are a direct reflection of a life of bondage and rebellion. They are sin, and must be repented for. An addiction is actually a misdirection of worship. Sometimes, it can have its root in seeds of emotional imprinting in a person's life.

k. **Rejection and Negative self-image** -- a person continually needs affirmation (more than is normal), and must have "self" fed, in order to feel accepted in any degree. Rejection has a spiritual base, usually in the past of the individual, and memories have formed a type of mold for the personality to follow. (See Proverbs 15:4, Proverbs 18:21)

Pray for revelation knowledge of the Love of Father God to penetrate the wall of rejection. (See Romans 8:35-39, and Isaiah 54:17) Also, a more in-depth ministry, such as "Lessons for Liberty," (available through Awakenedtogrow.com, can equip the person for victorious Christian Life.

l. **Immoral Sexual Behavior** – An appetite for perversion

(See I Corinthians 6:16-18, Romans 6:23) Death comes in three forms – physical emotional and spiritual.

m. **Spirits of Death** – whether outwardly directed or inwardly directed. This is a murderous spirit towards others – suicidal when directed inward (See Psalm 118:17-19, and Isaiah 38:18-19)

n. **Occultic involvement** – Anything related to the occult (Deuteronomy 18 and 19) astrology, reading horoscopes, palm reading, Ouija boards, tarot cards, séances, fortune telling, witchcraft, divination, sorcery, magic, casting spells, casting hexes, voodoo, secret societies, etc.) Even if you don't take it seriously, evil spirits do.

Sometimes, a person can have something in their possession innocently, that is an abomination to the Lord, and not know it. Seek God into prayer, and ask the Lord to show you room by room what you need to "clean out" of your home. (Good examples: face masks from the West Indies or Africa, Greek mythological materials, American Indian tribal items, anything with deities from "other religions") See Deuteronomy 7:25

Session Eight – Homework

1. Please complete any reading you are behind in to this point, this week.

2. Utilize this week to get your journaling and writing assignments on track with the level of assignment this week. Complete the worksheets you have been given so far.

3. Complete your Bible reading that has not been completed so far, and work to memorize the verses assigned in the program so far.

Session Eight – Personal Discovery Journal

Mentoring Assignment #8
Taking Hold of the Promises, Part B

1. If you have not already done so, please take a moment to look over the past five assignments we have completed together. Refer to the instructions at the beginning of Assignment 5. Please be sure before moving forward, that you have completed your imprinting description of who God is to you – Someone you can relate to; based upon the Scriptures.

   Read over your description of the nature of Father God – add to it anything that has ministered specifically to you in session seven, or in this session. What are you learning about how God feels about you? Can you allow the love of God into your heart on this new and deeper level?

2. Now we come to the subject of trust. It is absolutely essential in our spiritual and emotional growth as believers that we develop the ability to be transparent, honest, open and trusting not only of the Holy Spirit, but also of each other within the body of Christ. The choice to become a risk-taker, who places trust outside of oneself requires a great deal of courage and must be driven by a desire to grow into spiritual maturing more than anything else in life.

Are you willing to begin the journey to trust the Lord Jesus completely with your heart, and let Him bring you to full maturity? Reaffirm that choice here.

_____

3. Remember:

When we begin to trust, it is important that we realize that before we are able to trust any other person, we must first become able to fully trust Jesus to take care of us. Please utilize the following scriptures. After looking up the scripture in the left hand column, please give a description of the trustworthiness of Jesus in the right hand column.

Scripture	Description
Psalm 121 -- *I will lift up my eyes to the hills— From whence comes my help? My help comes from the LORD, Who made heaven and earth. He will not allow your foot to be moved; He who keeps you will not slumber. Behold, He who keeps Israel Shall neither slumber nor sleep. The LORD is your keeper; The LORD is your shade at your right hand. The sun shall not strike you by day, Nor the moon by night. The LORD shall preserve you from all evil; He shall preserve your soul. The LORD shall preserve your going out and your coming in from this time forth, and even forevermore.*	
Psalm 147:11	
Proverbs 3:5-6 -- *Trust in the LORD with all your heart, And lean not on your own understanding -- In all your ways acknowledge Him and He shall direct your paths.*	
Proverbs 14:26	
Proverbs 28:25 – (The Message) -- *A grasping person stirs up trouble, but trust in GOD brings a sense of well-being.*	
Proverbs 29:25	

Scripture	Description
Isaiah 25:1 -- *O LORD, You are my God. I will exalt You, I will praise Your name, For You have done wonderful things; Your counsels of old are faithfulness and truth.*	
Isaiah 26:3	
Isaiah 49:15-16 -- *Can a woman forget her nursing child, And not have compassion on the son of her womb? Surely they may forget, Yet I will not forget you. See, I have inscribed you on the palms of My hands; Your walls are continually before Me.*	
Isaiah 54:10	
Jeremiah 17:7-8 -- *Blessed is the man who trusts in the LORD, And whose hope is the LORD. For he shall be like a tree planted by the waters, Which spreads out its roots by the river, and will not fear when heat comes; But its leaf will be green, and will not be anxious in the year of drought, nor will cease from yielding fruit.*	
Jeremiah 33:20-21	
Lamentations 3:22-23 -- *Through the LORD's mercies we are not consumed, because His compassions fail not. They are new every morning; Great is Your faithfulness.*	
Daniel 9:4	
Hosea 2:19-20 -- *I will betroth you to Me forever; Yes, I will betroth you to Me in righteousness and justice, in lovingkindness and mercy; I will betroth you to Me in faithfulness, and you shall know the LORD.*	

Scripture	**Description**

Nahum 1:7 -- *The LORD is good, A stronghold in the day of trouble; and He knows those who trust in Him.*

Matthew 24:35

I Corinthians 2:5 -- *that your faith should not be in the wisdom of men but in the power of God.*

I Corinthians 10:13

II Corinthians 1:20-- *For all the promises of God in Him (in Jesus) are Yes, and in Him Amen, to the glory of God through us.*

I Thessalonians 5:24

II Timothy 2:11-13 -- *This is a faithful saying: For if we died with Him, we shall also live with Him. If we endure, We shall also reign with Him. If we deny Him, He also will deny us. If we are faithless, He remains faithful; He cannot deny Himself.*

Hebrews 6:18

Hebrews 10:23 -- *Let us hold fast the confession of our hope without wavering, for He who promised is faithful.*

Hebrews 10:38-39

Scripture	**Description**

Hebrews 11:1-6 -- *Faith means being sure of the things we hope for and knowing that something is real even if we do not see it. Faith is the reason we remember great people who lived in the past. It is by faith we understand that the whole world was made by God's command so what we see was made by something that cannot be seen. It was by faith that Abel offered God a better sacrifice than Cain did. God said he was pleased with the gifts Abel offered and called Abel a good man because of his faith. Abel died, but through his faith he is still speaking. It was by faith that Enoch was taken to heaven so he would not die. He could not be found, because God had taken him away. Before he was taken, the Scripture says that he was a man who truly pleased God. Without faith no one can please God. Anyone who comes to God must believe that he is real and that he rewards those who truly want to find him.*

Hebrews 13:6

II Peter 3:9 -- *The Lord is not slow in doing what he promised—the way some people understand slowness. But God is being patient with you. He does not want anyone to be lost, but he wants all people to change their hearts and lives.*

I John 5:4

4. What fears you have battled with in the past were addressed by the statements about Abba Father in these scriptures? List them here.

5. Can you choose to trust, completely and without question, the representative of the Person of Jesus Christ that the Holy Spirit has made real to you through these assignments?

6. Please spend some time in prayer, perhaps with a friend to agree with you, witnessing and supporting your decision to confront these issues in your life. Pray together regarding your choice to become open, honest and vulnerable with the Lord Jesus in these new areas of your life. Make confession, and repent for the areas of your life in which you chose your own way. Ask the Holy Spirit to strengthen your will to be able to choose to believe the Word of God, and what Jesus has to say regarding spiritual life, more than you believe your own feelings, emotions, and perceptions.

Suggestions of what to repent and seek freedom from:
(This prayer signifies the desire to walk away from these life patterns)

Suspicion of male authority
Distrust and fear of male authority
Hatred of men
Anger, and self-vindication
Independence of spirit and attitude
Control – the desire to rule oneself
Lack of inner submission
Believing the perceptions of the past
Withdrawal and inner retreat
Neglect of the Word of God
Not applying the Word of God
Manipulation of circumstances
Gossip, slander, sins of the tongue
Following your own path
Setting the standard for others
Criticism (this would even the field in your mind, when you felt inadequate in the past)
Being selfish
Being self-centered
Serving yourself before you served others
Unwillingness to pursue relationships with other women
Neglect of bonding in relationships

7. Now that you have spiritually removed the barriers to trusting Jesus as an authority figure, realize that Abba Father will take you at your word, and will begin the work of healing in your heart. As you give Him the time and room to do this healing, it is important you reinforce the choices you have made with prayer and Bible study. Please try to pray for 10 minutes – whether in worship, or in prayer times each day from this point on in your life. Also, pray in the Spirit, utilizing your spiritual language for 5 minutes each day. If this is difficult for you to do at first, set a kitchen timer as you begin each prayer segment, and pray until it goes off.

Please utilize these note pages as you listen to the recorded lecture for Session Nine.

Ruth and Naomi – The Healing Journey
Session Nine – The Shaping of Personality

"G.E.M.S." Personality Assessment Profile

Please circle a 0, 1, 2, or 3, next to each statement below, using the following legend:

at all   1 = rarely   2 = sometimes   3 = always

1. I never can understand why people don't just use common sense.   0 1 2 3   (G)

2. I am at my best when I can work with others in a fun environment.   0 1 2 3   (M)

3. People who know me, say I am a continual ball of energy.   0 1 2 3   (M)

4. When I am a friend to someone, I should loyal no matter what.   0 1 2 3   (E)

5. I like to think things through before I begin a project.   0 1 2 3   (S)

6. I like to speak my mind, and let the "chips fall where they will."   0 1 2 3   (G)

7. I like to tell jokes and funny stories.   0 1 2 3   (M)

8. I try to avoid conflict whenever possible.   0 1 2 3   (E)(S)

9. I like to research and analyze details.   0 1 2 3   (S)

10. I think people should know what to do in an emergency.   0 1 2 3   (G)(S)

11. Rules keep everyone safe, and make things fair.   0 1 2 3   (E)

12. I feel that Spontaneity is important; it prevents boredom.   0 1 2 3   (M)

13. I would rather work alone than with others.   0 1 2 3   (G)(S)

14. I try to be supportive of those in my sphere of influence.   0 1 2 3   (E)

15. I hate being used, or having someone take advantage of me.   0 1 2 3   (G)

16. Sometimes I feel so disorganized.   0 1 2 3   (M)

17. When I get hurt, I tend to withdraw.   0 1 2 3   (E)

18. I think rules and boundaries should be challenged.   0 1 2 3   (G)

19. When I am in a disagreement with someone, I need to clarify.   0 1 2 3   (S)

20. When I am in a group, I tend to be quiet.   0 1 2 3   (E)

21. I tend to be persistent.   0 1 2 3   (G)(S)

22. I have been told I have a dry sense of humor.   0 1 2 3   (E)

23. I don't know why some people have to be so practical.   0 1 2 3   (M)

24. I struggle with suspicion sometimes.   0 1 2 3   (S)

25. I feel sorry for people when they are hurting. I want to help.   0 1 2 3   (E)(M)

26. I tend to feel deeply, and maintain fully invested relationships.   0 1 2 3   (E)

27. I take pride in being a dependable person.   0 1 2 3   (E)

28. I tend to be a perfectionist.   0 1 2 3   (S)

29. I tend to be decisive and goal-oriented.   0 1 2 3   (G)

30. It is hard work for me to concentrate on just one thing.	0 1 2 3	(M)
31. I tend to take charge when others lag behind.	0 1 2 3	(G)
32. It is very important to me that I be understood.	0 1 2 3	(E)(S)
33. I am deeply wounded when I am overlooked.	0 1 2 3	(M)
35. I think I should be rewarded when I achieve a goal.	0 1 2 3	(G)
36. Life should be fun.	0 1 2 3	(M)
37. I need to experience respect from others in relationship.	0 1 2 3	(G)(M)
38. I am usually right.	0 1 2 3	(G)
39. I need to know that I have freedom to make my own decisions.	0 1 2 3	(S)
40. It is important to me to know that others accept me.	0 1 2 3	(E)(M)
41. I would rather receive respect from others than approval.	0 1 2 3	(G)(E)
42. I need to feel close, and intimate with the people I care about.	0 1 2 3	(S)
43. When people ignore my efforts, or don't notice them, I get hurt.	0 1 2 3	(S)
44. It is important that people have a goal, or nothing will be done.	0 1 2 3	(G)
45. I wish people would control their attitudes and anger.	0 1 2 3	(E)
46. I have a tendency to worry.	0 1 2 3	(E)(S)

47. I tend to get away to a quiet place without people to recharge.   0 1 2 3   (S)

48. I hate to be alone.   0 1 2 3   (M)

49. Its hard to hurt my feelings.   0 1 2 3   (M)(G)

50. I battle with insecurity in social situations.   0 1 2 3   (S)

51. Conflict makes me nervous.   0 1 2 3   (E)(S)

52. Others consider me to be an outgoing person.   0 1 2 3   (G)(M)

53. When a situation gets too serious or intense, I lighten it up.   0 1 2 3   (M)

54. I am comfortable setting boundaries with demanding people.   0 1 2 3   (G)

55. I am uncomfortable with changes happening quickly.   0 1 2 3   (E)

Please tally your totals here. For questions that have two letters next to the indicator, add the points to the tally for both letters.

G____   E____   M____   S____

The highest scoring sections indicate your most prevalent personality styles. See the following pages for help in understanding what each personality style means. For a more detailed assessment, see the GEMS Personal Discovery Tool, by Debbye Graafsma; (available on lulu.com or amazon.com). The GEMS Assessment helps in deciphering Gifts, Empowerment, Maturity and Serving values. It is available on amazon.com, lulu.com and through awakenedtogrow.com.

"G.E.M.S." Personality Assessment Profiles

G -Golden Eagle

Golden Eagles, *recognized as leaders in the raptor world, are solitary birds, living in grassland areas. Their nests are constructed of sticks, formed into a bowl, and built in high elevations like a cliff ledge or a high tree. Unlike other eagles, Goldens will not eat carrion unless there is no other food source to be found. This makes them extremely healthy as raptors. Golden Eagles are fiercely territorial, very persistent, and single focused. In teaching their young to fly, they will practice a drop/catch/bear-up/repeat pattern, until the fledgling is able to stay in flight. They mate for life. They are the largest of all raptors, with a wingspan of up to 7 feet. Newly hatched chicks are covered with pure white, downy feathers.*

E -Emerald Dove

Emerald Doves, *recognized as loyal and social creatures, fly in tight formation during the breeding season, in a beautiful collective display. These birds are committed and reliable. They form flocks, and are very calm and gentle in nature. They avoid busy atmospheres, and soothe their mate and their young with a soft "coo-ing" sound. They can survive in desert as well as urban environments. They are able to eat 20% of their body weight in a day, storing seed until they can digest it later. They can live as long as 30 years. Most flocks of this specie follow a predictable and repeated pattern in their living pattern. Emerald doves usually occur singly, pairs or in small groups. They are quite terrestrial, often searching for fallen fruit on the ground and spending little time in trees except when roosting.*

M -Macaroni Penguin

Macaroni Penguins, *are recognized as fun-loving and energetic. They can live as long as 20 years. They are found south of the equator, and, although they tend to inhabit islands and remote landmasses that are free of land predators, these little guys spend as much as 75% of their life at sea. They do not fly, but when swimming, their wings flap underwater, just as other birds in the air. Penguins like to play; to "toboggan" on their bellies on hills of ice or snow. Penguins communicate by vocalizing and performing physical behaviors called "displays". They use many vocal and visual displays to communicate nesting territories and mating information. They also use displays in partner and chick recognition, and in defense against intruders. Penguins are very conscious to keep their feathers coated with personal oils, and they preen continually.*

S -Solitary African Weaver

Solitary African Weavers *are considered creative and detail-oriented. They are among the bird world's best architects. A large grassy nest usually contains several rooms, which the bird enters from below. The weaver lines the branches leading to the nest and the nest itself with thorny twigs as a defense against predators. The Solitary Weaver, unlike others in its specie, tends to isolate away from others. They work creatively and continuously, building multiple nests in a single breeding season. The male is brightly colored, usually in red or yellow and black. Weavers have been given their name because of their elaborately woven nests. Materials used for building nests include fine leaf-fibers, grass, and twigs.*

G	**E**	**M**	**S**
Golden Eagle 	**Emerald Dove** 	**Macaroni Penguin** 	**Solitary Weaver** 
Strengths(Open) born leader, dynamic, active, works well with change, must correct wrongs, strong-willed, decisive, not ruled by emotions, confident, organized, not easily discouraged, independent, delegates well, goals-driven, stimulates others, doesn't fear opposition, motivates others, is usually right, excels in emergencies, moves quickly to action. Recharges alone.	*Strengths(Open)* low keyed, easygoing & relaxed, calm, cool, and collected, patient, well-balanced, consistent life, quiet by witty, sympathetic, kind, keeps emotions hidden, happily reconciled to life, all-purpose person, competent and steady, peaceful, agreeable, administrative ability, avoids conflicts, finds the easy way, takes time for others, is not in a hurry, takes the good with the bad, doesn't get upset easily, easy to get along with, pleasant and enjoyable, inoffensive, good listener, dry sense of humor, enjoys watching people, has many friends, has compassion and concern, loyal, trustworthy	*Strengths(Open)* appealing, good storyteller, good sense of humor, memory for color, life of the party, holds attention, emotional, demonstrative, curious, wide-eyed, innocent, good on stage, changeable disposition, lives for the present, always a child, very sincere, makes home fun, turns disaster into humor, "circus master," makes friend easily, loves people, thrives on compliments, volunteers readily, has energy and enthusiasm, inspires others to join, charms others to work, creative and colorful, apologizes quickly, likes spontaneity, doesn't hold grudges.	*Strengths(Open)* deep & thoughtful, serious, analytical, purposeful, genius prone, designer, creative, philosophical, poetic, sensitive to others, self-sacrificing, conscientious, idealistic, schedule oriented, sets high standards, detail conscious, persistent and thorough, orderly, organized, economical, solver, driven to finish, likes chart-maker, picks up after others, wants things done well, encourages scholarship, makes friends cautiously, content to stay in background, avoids causing attention, faithful and devoted, will listen, deep concern for others, seeks ideal mate.
Needs to be respected. *Fears being used or taken advantage of.* *In communication: needs the other person to "get to the point."*	*Needs to be included.* *Fears losing their sense of security and safety.* *In communication: needs the other person "to take the anger out of it; be nice to me."*	*Needs to be heard and validated.* *Fears ridicule and being left alone.* *In communication; needs to know they are heard and understood*	*Needs to be appreciated and encouraged.* *Fears criticism and rejection.* *In communication; puts great weight on words; needs assurance*

# G	# E	# M	# S
Golden Eagle 	**Emerald Dove** 	**Macaroni Penguin** 	**Solitary Weaver** 
Wall Elements Pride, Emotional unavailability. Tendency towards narcissism	*Wall Elements* Rejection, Fear, Tendency towards co-dependency.	*Wall Elements* Pride, Emotional unavailability. Tendency towards addictions/ co-dependency.	*Wall Elements* Fear, Negative Emotion, Tendency towards Isolation/Narcissism.
Weaknesses(Closed)	**Weaknesses(Closed)**	**Weaknesses(Closed)**	**Weaknesses(Closed)**
bossy, impatient, quick-temper, can't relax, impetuous, enjoys arguing, won't give up when losing, comes on too strong, is not complimentary, inflexible, dislikes emotions/tears, no tolerance for mistakes, unsympathetic, demands loyalty, can be rude/tactless, tends to dominate, too busy for family, gives quick answers, won't let others relax, uses others, knows everything, decides for others, can do everything "better," is too independent, possessive, doesn't apologize, might be right, but unpopular	unenthusiastic, fearful & worried, indecisive, avoids responsibility, quietly stubborn, selfish, too shy, retreating, self-righteous, not goal oriented, lacks motivation, hard to get moving, resents being pushed, lazy and careless, discourages others, would rather watch, lax on discipline, doesn't organize, takes like too easy, dampens others' enthusiasm, stays uninvolved, is not exciting or excitable, indifferent to plans, judges others, sarcastic and teasing, resists change	compulsive talker, exaggerates, dwells on trivia, forgets details, scares others off, too happy, restless energy, egotistical, gets angry easily, blusters/complains, seems phony, never grows up, forgets obligations, doesn't follow through, undisciplined, priorities out of order, easily distracted, disorganized, doesn't hear the whole story, hates to be alone, needs center stage, popular, looks for credit, dominates conversations, interrupts and doesn't listen, answers for others, makes excuses, repeats stories, fickle, keeps home in a frenzy, decides by feelings, confidence fades quickly	remembers the negatives, moody and depressed, enjoys being hurt, has false humility, off in another world, low self-image, has selective hearing, self-centered, too introspective, guilt feelings, persecution complex, tends to hypochondria, not people oriented, depressed over imperfections, chooses difficult work, hesitant to begin projects, spends too much time planning, prefers analysis to working, hard to please, self-depreciating, unaffectionate, standards/expectations are too high, deep need for approval, puts goals out of reach, discourages others, too meticulous, becomes martyr, sulks over disagreements, lives through others, insecure socially, withdrawn and remote, critical, suspicious dislikes those in opposition, antagonistic, vengeful, skeptical of compliments, full of contradictions

How Personality Blends in Relationships

Extrovert and Activity Based

"I will lead you to get it done."

"Golden Eagle"
"Driver"
"Choleric"
"Lion"

DECISIVE
LEADER

Motivated by: making the choices, seeking how it benefits personal goals

Task oriented styles

"Solitary Weaver"
"Conscientious"
"Melancholic"
"Beaver"

THINKER
WORKER, ANALYTICAL

"It must be done well, and planned well."

Introvert and Security Based

Motivated by: understanding the "whys" Affirmation and encouragement

Extrovert and Activity Based

"Let's have fun while we get it done."

"Macaroni Penguin"
"Inspirer"
"Sanguine"
"Otter"

TALKER
LOTS OF FUN

Motivated by: social opportunities, activity, ability to share thoughts

CONFLICT

Relationship oriented styles

"Emerald Dove"
"Steady"
"Phlegmatic"
"Golden Retriever"

LOYAL
EVEN TEMPERED

"Don't worry. We will get it done together."

Introvert and Stationery Based

Motivated by: consistency, seeing benefit to others; how serves common goal

Session Nine – Homework

1. Please continue your reading book, and make notes of the discoveries and questions you are encountering as you read.

2. If new memories come to mind regarding male authority figures, add them to the journal entries you completed during the last session. Finish the assignment of deciphering your perceptions and inner life judgments.

3. What is your basic personality? What is the personality of those who have wounded you? Were there conflicts in those relationships? Take a moment to consider how the conflicts may have been fueled to become traumatic in your life. Make note of those relationships that were weak due to an inability to connect on a level of personality….. allow your heart to receive the approval of Abba Father – He created you with the personality you have…. He likes you.

4. Finish your memorization assignments to this point in the program.

5. Psalm 103: 8 -- "The Lord is gracious, full of compassion, slow to anger, and great in mercy." Please also read Ephesians, chapter five and six this week.

6. Please complete the worksheets you have not yet completed, and finish your Imprinting Description of Father God.

Session Nine –
Personal Discovery Journal

Mentoring Assignment #9
Addressing Broken Trust, Part A

1. The repairing of broken trust is something that is multi-faceted in its development. First, the choice to become vulnerable must be made, in regard to the healing process. It is necessary that you choose, now, in this session, to let your heart become open and vulnerable --

   First --   **with Jesus,** in the representation the Holy Spirit
                   has made real to your heart.

   Second --   **with your mentor**, because she has been provided as a
                   safe place for you – a support, an encouragement, and to
                   help you when the process hits on difficult places.

   Third --   **with your pastoral trainer**, because she has been
                   provided as a safe place for your mentor, and for you
                   as you walk through these new areas of growth and
                   commitment.

Fill out this prayer of commitment and choice here, in regard to taking the steps to repair broken trust in your life.

"Father God, today (date) _____, I choose to trust You, because you are my (image He has made real to you) _____. You are my Rescuer, my Helper, my Comfort, and my Counselor, and You are using this process to set me free from the wounds that Satan has brought against my life.

Father God, additionally, I choose to trust those women you have placed in my life to help me grow through the rough places I have encountered. I know that You have given them to me as a safe place for healing and wholeness. I specifically name (mentor)_____ and (pastoral trainer) _____ _____. I choose to allow You to help me to open my heart, and become vulnerable, enabling growth in new areas of my life.

I love you, Jesus, and I trust you to help me to choose the right path, as you rebuild areas of trust in my life. Help me to grow. I need you. Amen."

Please read this prayer out loud, making confession with your own mouth of the steps you are taking to grow. Then write out your own prayer of commitment and choice here.

_____

_____

_____

_____

_____

_____

Please meet with a friend, or prayer partner, to agree together, pray for this next step of development in your life.

Please read James 5:13-16.

a. In verse 13, who does Jesus say is responsible to pray?

___

b. In verse 14, who does Jesus say is responsible to call for the elders, establishing prayer for healing?

___

c. In verse 15, who is does Jesus say is responsible to ask for forgiveness for sins that might have brought on sickness?

___

d. In the same way, in verse 16, what action promotes healing?

___

So, in order to grow spiritually and emotionally, in this process of development, it is your responsibility to express the need. The enemy of our souls tells us that God doesn't care about us, or that leadership doesn't care, because we are not pursued when we have difficulty. Satan wants you to believe that no one loves you, and that there is no hope for you. But those are lies, fabricated to keep you from becoming the person you were destined to be. (And yes, we all have a destined purpose!! – don't buy that one either!!)

The problem is that when we begin listening to Satan's lies, we choose passivity, and we stop growing. And all Father God is waiting for, is for us to make confession of our need, and ask for help.

Did you know that every scripture that holds promise in it, is written with you in mind?

Write out Romans 2:10 and 11 here.

_____
_____
_____
_____
_____
_____
_____
_____

Please read Hebrews 13:9

What strengthens the heart? _____

Please describe what grace is here. If you have difficulty coming up with a description, please talk to your mentor.

_____
_____
_____
_____
_____

What promises has Father God given to you, personally, in His Word? List them here, in the left column, and then put in writing, in the right hand column, what you believe has been promised to you.

Scripture	**Promise**

Please utilize these note pages as you listen to the recorded lecture for Session Ten.

Ruth and Naomi – The Healing Journey
Session Ten – The Patterns of Safe Community

To Abuse – *to use wrongfully, engage in hurtful practice, to destroy identity or inner life within an individual*

Note: 95% of all domestic abuse is targeted at the wife. For this reason, this chart refers to the abused as "her."

The Abuse Wheel

Power And Control

YELLING/SCREAMING Overpowering with volume and will when communicating
USING COERCION & THREATS Making and/or carrying out threats to do something to hurt your spouse * threatening to leave her, to commit suicide, to report her to welfare * making her drop charges * making her do illegal things

PHYSICAL VIOLENCE – any touch without permission used to gain agreement when communicating
USING INTIMIDATION Making her afraid by using looks, actions, gestures * smashing things * destroying her property * abusing pets * displaying weapons * invading her comfort zone and using your size to get her to yield

USING ECONOMIC ABUSE
* Preventing her from getting or keeping a job * Making her ask for money *Giving her an allowance *Taking her money *Not letting her know about or have access to family income. *Not sharing your income, and keeping it for your own activities.

USING EMOTIONAL ABUSE
* Putting her down *Saying unkind things * Making her feel bad about herself * Calling her names * making her think she's crazy * playing mind games * humiliating her * having relationships with other women on trust levels that are designed to be for her alone *using guilt and shame to motivate her

USING MALE PRIVILEGE
* Treating her like a servant, no household help with organization or chores – "provider mindset" *Making all the big decisions * Acting like the "master of the castle" *Being the one to define men's & women's roles * Spiritualizing the abuse, and calling it "submission." * Intentionally keeping her pregnant.

USING ISOLATION
* Controlling what she does, who she sees and talks to, what she reads, where she goes.
* Limiting her outside involvement
* Using jealousy to justify actions.

USING CHILDREN
* Making her feel guilty about the children * Using the children to relay messages * Using visitation to harass her * Threatening to take the children away from her.

MINIMALIZING, DENYING AND BLAMING
* Making light of the abuse and not taking her concerns about it seriously * Saying the abuse didn't happen * Shifting the responsibility for the abusive behavior * Saying she caused it, or she deserved it

SEXUAL ABUSE – Waking her up for sex; stimulation to bring response against her will
* Using her physical response to satisfy your own need, without regard for her emotions *Taking without giving lingering care or love-making *When sex is the only form of intimacy * Rape= sex against her will *Acting out Pornography *Forced abortion *Prostitution *Party sex

© 2006 ATG/dcg

To Parent – *to bond with a child on the level of trust at a deep level, imparting life skills for independent development and trustworthy citizenship as a later adult.*

Note: The responsibility for taking the initiation to bond in a parent/child relationship falls to the parent. It is action, born out of love and/or choice.

The Healthy Parenting Wheel

Healthy Parenting and/or Mentoring

ACTIVE LISTENING and NEGOTIATION
*Speaking kindly and with words that build relationship *Listening to the child's point of view without immediately correcting or criticizing.

PROVIDING TO SEE NEEDS MET
* Helping your child to resolve inner conflicts, through discovery
* Accepting and making changes
* Being willing to give ground.
*Not having to be "right," or have the last word, unless it is a safety issue.

ECONOMIC TRAINING
* Making money decisions together, teaching the child to manage earned money well, with tithing coming before purchase goals.
* Teaching the child to be a giver, by modeling the example.
*Equally sharing and contributing earnings for the common good.

BEING A SAFE PERSON –
Communicating safe touch, in safe areas, without invading privacy or comfort zone. Not intimidating a child, or threatening, even in silence.

CREATING A SAFE PLACE --
Talking and acting in such a way that the child feels safe and is comfortable in expression
*Inviting, participation in activities. * Being genuinely interested in what the child feels and has to say.

RESPECT
* Listening to the child without judgment— guiding with questions * Being emotionally affirming and understanding. * Discipline for child's inner life development; not because of personal frustration or embarrassment. *Being emotionally available * Valuing opinions, views and feelings. * Not being offended by disagreement, but seeking to teach for change.

SHARING RESPONSIBILITIES
* Agreeing to and following through on a fair distribution of work in the home, teaching the child to work for rewards
* Allowing the child to contribute to family decisions when possible.
* Teaching the child to be a worker and a helper, not just to receive.
* Being truly spiritual, serving in the home as unto the Lord, modeling mutual submission.

BEING A REPONSIBLE PARENT
* Sharing parenting responsibilities equally
* Being a positive, encouraging, non-violent role model and mentor for the children.
* Bonding to the children

BEING HONEST And ACCOUNTABLE
* Accepting responsibility for your own actions
* Acknowledging your past usage of violence and/or abuse.
*Admitting being wrong, asking for forgiveness, making amends. Not repeating the abuse.
* Communicating openly and truthfully.

TRUSTING and SUPPORTING
* Encouraging the child to discover their giftings, and to follow God-given goals in life.
* Respecting the child's own feelings, friends, activities and opinions.
*Believing in their dreams and abilities, and shaping values regarding Father's plan for those dreams.

SEXUAL HEALTH –
*Bringing identity issues into the light *Talking about needs and learning together, without demands.
*Answering questions the child asks without fear or avoidance, with honest appropriate for the age level.
* Allow child to see you hug and express care. Being willing talk about emotions.

© 2006 ATG/dcg

To Marry – *to trust another person with your life on a deep level, bonding to the point of the creation of a new and joint identity.*

The Healthy Marriage Wheel

EQUALITY in Relationship

ACTIVE LISTENING and NEGOTIATION
* Speaking kindly and with words that build relationship
* Listening to each other's point of view without interruption or judgment, or defensiveness.

PARTNERING TO SEE NEEDS MET
* Seeking mutually satisfying answers to conflicts & disagreements
* Accepting and making changes
* Being willing to give ground.
* Not having to be "right," or have the last word.

BEING A SAFE PERSON –
Asking before touching, especially in areas pre-disposed to pain.

CREATING A SAFE PLACE --
Talking and acting in such a way that she feels safe and is comfortable expressing herself.
* Inviting, without expectation, her participation in activities.
* Being genuinely interested in what she feels and has to say.

RESPECTING HER
* Listening to her without judgment
* Being emotionally affirming and understanding.
* Being emotionally available
* Valuing her opinions, views and feelings.
* Allowing her to disagree with you, without becoming offended

ECONOMIC PARTNERSHIP
* Making money decisions together, viewing each one's viewpoint as vital and important.
* Being sure that everyone benefits from financial arrangements.
* Equally sharing and contributing earnings for the common good.

SHARING RESPONSIBILITIES
* Agreeing to and following through on a fair distribution of work in the home.
* Making family decisions together, as a team.
* Defining roles together, and being willing to help each other.
* Being truly spiritual, serving in the home as unto the Lord, with mutual submission.

BEING A RESPONSIBLE PARENT
* Sharing parenting responsibilities equally
* Being a positive, encouraging, non-violent role model and mentor for the children.
* Bonding to the children

BEING HONEST And ACCOUNTABLE
* Accepting responsibility for your own actions
* Acknowledging your past usage of violence and/or abuse.
* Admitting being wrong, asking for forgiveness, making amends. Not repeating the abuse.
* Communicating openly and truthfully.

TRUSTING and SUPPORTING
* Encouraging her to follow her goals in life.
* Respecting her right to have her own feelings, friends, activities and opinions.
* Believing in her dreams and abilities.

SEXUAL HEALTH –
* Bringing identity issues into the light
* Talking about needs and learning together, without demands.
* Mutually giving to each other, without fear.
* Honest communication regarding enjoyment
* More about giving love, than getting satisfaction.
* More about emotional intimacy than body contact, stimulation or gratification

© 2006 ATG/dcg

Session Ten – Homework

1. Please continue reading your supplemental reading book, and make notes of your discoveries, and questions.

2. Please complete the worksheets on the following pages. As you do so, complete the worksheets on the following pages, make note of the promises Abba Father has made about His character that speak to your heart. Are there areas where you could make determination to choose to believe He is safe in His care for you? As you contemplate these things, journal your discoveries.

3. Please read Psalm 103 each night this week before you go to sleep. Before you close your eyes, ask the Holy Spirit to give you a deeper awareness of the God who is described in this chapter.

4. Please memorize Romans 15:13:

    "Now may the God of hope fill you with all joy and peace in believing, that you may abound in hope by the power of the Holy Spirit." Romans 15:13

Session Ten –
Personal Discovery Journal

Mentoring Assignment #10
God's Balance Sheet of Forgiveness

Please turn to Matthew 18:21-35. Read the story, and then answer the questions below.

a. verse 23   Who was responsible to settle the accounts?

---

b. verse 24-25   The first slave owed more than $10 million in silver to his master. Even if he and his family were separated and sold, the price they would draw could not come anywhere close to that much. (In earthly terms, the man owed more than his life was worth.)

c. verse 26   Could the slave pay the debt, in reality?

---

d. verse 27   What were the steps of forgiveness, the king walked through? List them here.

   1.

   2.

   3.

e. verse 28   The second servant's debt was the equivalent of one day's wage. What blind spot did the first servant have?

_____

_____

Could he see the relationship between the debt the second servant owed him, and his own debt that had been forgiven?

_____

f. verse 29-30   Was the first servant's heart open to the man who owed him the debt of one day's wage?

_____

   Was he grateful, really, for his own debt being forgiven?

_____

How can you tell?

What would have shown his gratitude?

g. verse 31-25   How does the king view the first servant's injustice in his dealings?

What did the king consider to have been a better representation of the king's action and attitude toward indebtedness?

What is the end result of the first slave's attitude of unforgiveness?

h. What areas in your own life have experienced torment? List them here.

9. Copy verse 35 here.

10. Now, take a moment and look back at the assignments you have completed in regard to journaling painful memories and experiences in your past.

From that assignment, please utilize the next few pages and make a list of the injuries, which have been speaking to your soul, and have been "in your face," in regard to pain and trust issues. Please make a bulleted list of those injuries in the left hand column below. Please also name the person who inflicted the injury with the memory, or painful circumstance. If the injury was due to a choice, which you made, please list yourself as the person who inflicted injury.

Injuries	Contrast assignment

Injuries	**Contrast assignment**

Injuries	Contrast assignment

11. Our own pain tends to blind us to the needs of others. And our pain is based upon our perception of the situation. Our perceptions are the basis of our reactions and choices.

It is important that we realize that we are not alone – ever. That even when things happen to us that were not the best possible situation – that when we bring that pain and difficulty to Father God, He is able to bring good out of it. He is able to heal. In order to facilitate that process – we must let go of our own perceptions, and allow Him to give us fresh insight and understanding.

Please look up the following scriptures, and please contrasting character qualities that pertain to Father God in the "Contrast Assignment" column, as they relate to the injuries you have listed.

The Scriptures are:

I Corinthians 13
Psalm 103
Psalm 91
Psalm 54:4-5
Psalm 18
Ephesians 2:1-10

....

13. Meet with a prayer partner and walk through these areas of pain and difficulty, making confession of your heart attitude, and any struggles you may have with releasing the injustices of these situations. Ask your mentor to help you to understand what bondages and difficulties the person who hurt you might have been struggling with, and ask the Lord to give you compassion for them. This is the first step in learning to forgive.

Please utilize these note pages as you listen to the recorded lecture for Session Eleven.

Ruth and Naomi – The Healing Journey
Session Eleven – Assessing Emotional Development

1.    2.    3.   4.

1. _____
2. _____
3. _____
4. _____

Stages of Development

Notes

Stages of Surrender

Notes

© 2005, dcg/atg

Lewis Kohlberg's Stages of Moral/Emotional Development

Stage of Development	Stage of Discovery	Actual Practice
Level One—Pre-Moral		
	Stage One – Obedience and Punishment orientation	Automatic deference to a higher power or authority. Avoids trouble. Objective responsibility.
	Stage Two – Naïve and Ego Centered Orientation	Right action is the action which satisfies the self's needs/ occasionally other's needs. Values are relative to each person's needs and perspectives. Naïve efforts of exchange and reciprocity.
Level Two – Role Conformity		
(Moral values reside in performing the right role, in maintaining the conventional order, and expectancies of others as a value in its own right.)	Stage Three—Good boy/ good-girl orientation	Person is oriented to needing approval, to pleasing others. Conformity is stereotyped to majority and natural role behavior, image centered. Actions are evaluated on the basis of intentions.
	Stage Four – Authority and Social-Order-Maintaining orientation	Person is oriented to life according to "doing duty" and to showing respect for authority, maintaining the social order for its own sake. Learns to regard earned expectations of others. Differentiates actions out of a sense of obligation to rules from actions for generally "nice" or natural motives.

Level Three – Self-Accepted Moral Principles		
(Morality is defined in terms of conformity to shared standards, rights, or duties apart from supporting authority. The standards conformed to are internal, and actions are based on an inner process of thought and judgment concerning right and wrong.)	Stage Five – Contractual – legalistic orientation	Norms of right and wrong are defined in terms of laws or institutionalized rules. When a conflict arises between individual needs and law or contract, though sympathetic to the former, the person believes the latter must prevail because of its greater functional rationality for society, and for the majority will and welfare.
	Stage Six – The morality of individual principles of conscience	Life orientation is not only toward existing social rules, but also toward the conscience as a directing agent, mutual trust and respect, and principles of moral choice, involving logical consistencies. Action is controlled by internalized ideals that exert a pressure to act accordingly, regardless of the reactions of others in the immediate environment. If one acts otherwise, self-condemnation and guilt result.

© 2005, atg/dcg

The Principles of Change

1. There is always hope for change.

2. We cannot change what we do not acknowledge.

3. The primary ingredient of the change process is Truth (in love) in an open heart.

4. We cannot change others. We can only change ourselves.

5. Repentance is the only catalyst (beginning place) for change to occur.

6. Our inner brokenness is the beginning place for repentance, and therefore Change.

7. Changes we seek to make within ourselves without the help of the Holy Spirit, will never be permanent, because they are based in our own works and effort.

8. We cannot expect God to give grace or healing, when we are unwilling to repent.

12. Growth cannot happen without change.

13. Change will involve both forward and backward motion, always with our eyes fixed upon the goal of becoming like Christ.

14. The Doorway into the Change Process is guarded from the inside, by a person who must open the door from the inside. It cannot be forced open.

12. Change must be chosen, sometimes with struggle.

13. Change comes as a result of Training, not as a result of simply trying, using the same tools we have used in the past.

14. Change is a process. It takes time. What took years to tear down will require a season of hard work to redeem, repair and restore.

15. It takes intentional maintenance for change to remain.

©2005, dcg/atg

Session Eleven – Homework

1. Please continue reading your supplemental reading book, and make notes of your discoveries, and questions.

2. Please complete the worksheets on the following pages. As you complete the worksheets on the following pages, make note of the promises Abba Father has made about His character that speak to your heart. Are there areas where you could make determination to choose to believe He is safe in His care for you? As you contemplate these things, journal your discoveries.

3. Please read Psalm 91 each night this week before you go to sleep. Before you close your eyes, ask the Holy Spirit to give you a deeper awareness of the God who is described in this chapter.

4. Please memorize Colossians 3:12-17

So, as those who have been chosen of God, holy and beloved ,put on a heart of compassion, kindness, humility, gentleness and patience; bearing with one another, and forgiving each other, whoever has a complaint against anyone; just as the Lord forgave you, so also should you. Beyond all these things put on love, which is the perfect bond of unity. Let the peace of Christ rule in your hearts, to which indeed you were called in one body; and be thankful. Let the word of Christ richly dwell within you, with all wisdom teaching and admonishing one another with psalms and hymns and spiritual songs, singing with thankfulness in your hearts to God. Whatever you do in word or deed, do all in the name of the Lord Jesus, giving thanks through Him to God the Father.

Session Eleven – Personal Discovery Journal

Mentoring Assignment #11
Restorative Power

1. In every situation in which injury occurs, Satan has been at work to steal, kill and destroy. It is important when we are seeking healing and restoration, that we remember that not only were we injured in the situation which occurred, but many times, the person who inflicted the injury was also taken more fully into a bondage or a painful circumstance of their own.

In order to receive healing, it is necessary that we realize that injury is Satan's tool to render us ineffective and to stop us from realizing our destiny.

In order to grow, we must choose to step out into new areas of trust and relationship with Jesus. Even though trust may have been broken with other authority figures, WE CAN ALWAYS TRUST HIM!!

Look up Luke 23:33-34. What lesson can we learn about forgiveness from Jesus' statement?

_____

_____

_____

Now look up Galatians 2:20. How does what it says relate to this subject?

_____

_____

_____

_____

14. There are hindrances to our ability to forgive. They can be categorized in four sections.

    a. judgments and assessments we have made about others

    b. we feel we have the right to become the final authority for our own lives.

    c. Memories and perceptions we have about our own lives, and or own pain.

    d. Pain

On a separate piece of paper, please take the bulleted list you made of injuries, and categorize each one according to the four categories listed above.

15. Look up the following scriptures, and next to each one, write out how that scripture speaks to you in relationship to forgiveness.

Psalm 86:5

Luke 17:3-4

Mark 11:24-26

James 5:15-16

Isaiah 43:25

Isaiah 55:6-8

Jeremiah 31:34

Meet with a prayer partner, and take communion together. Repent for bitterness and hardness of heart in any of these areas, and release the right to hold a grudge into the Father's hands.

Please utilize these note pages as you listen to the recorded lecture for Session Twelve.

Ruth and Naomi – The Healing Journey
Session Twelve – Identity Formation

(for a more in-depth study into this subject, please see "Elements of Identity Formation" by Debbye Graafsma (available on lulu.com or amazon.com)

Principles of Destiny Fulfillment

Search me, O God, and know my heart; try me, and know my thoughts. And see if there be any wicked way in me, and lead me in the way everlasting."
Psalm 139:23-24

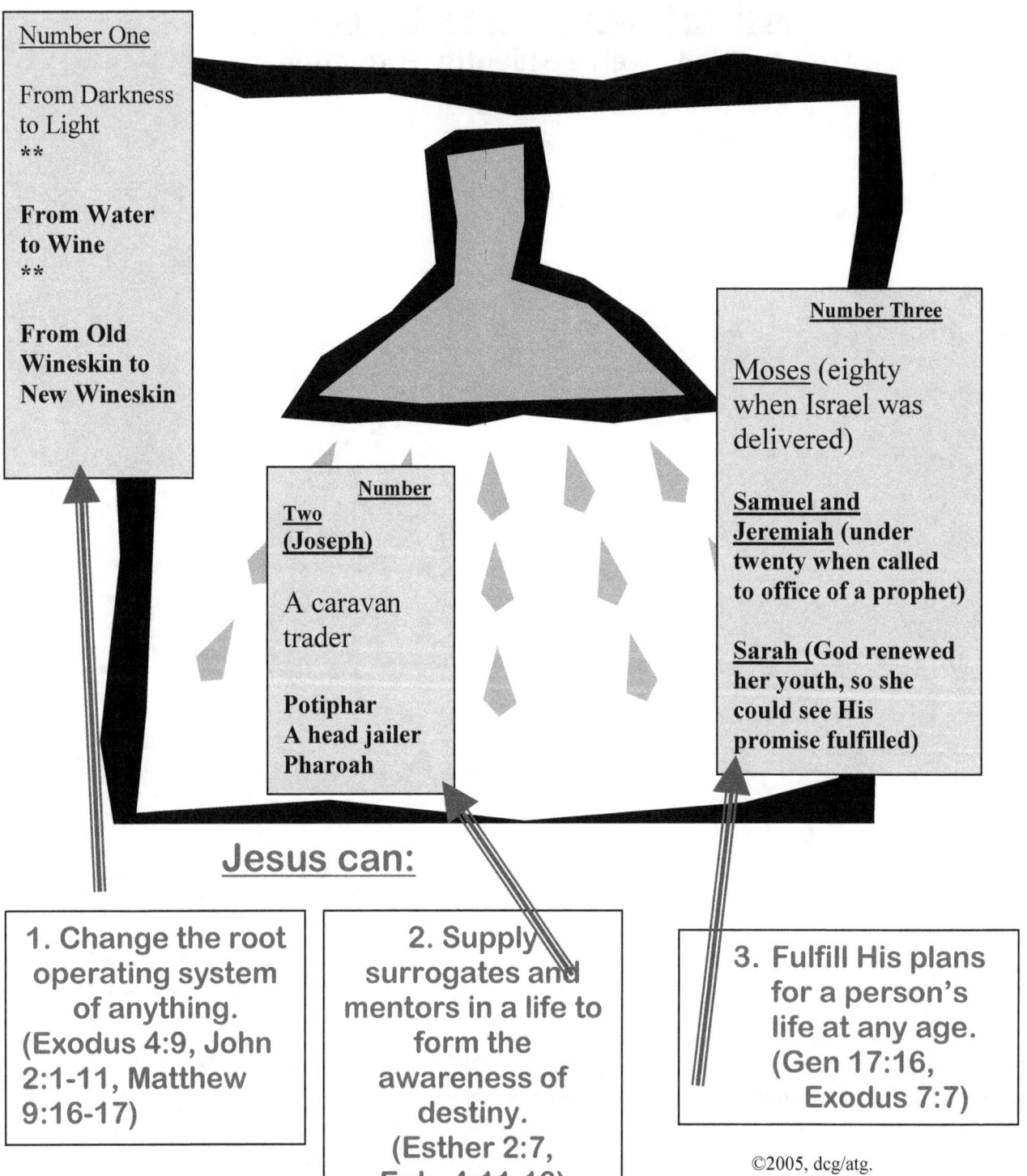

Number One

From Darkness to Light
**

From Water to Wine
**

From Old Wineskin to New Wineskin

Number Two (Joseph)

A caravan trader

Potiphar
A head jailer
Pharoah

Number Three

Moses (eighty when Israel was delivered)

Samuel and Jeremiah (under twenty when called to office of a prophet)

Sarah (God renewed her youth, so she could see His promise fulfilled)

Jesus can:

1. Change the root operating system of anything. (Exodus 4:9, John 2:1-11, Matthew 9:16-17)

2. Supply surrogates and mentors in a life to form the awareness of destiny. (Esther 2:7, Eph. 4:11-16)

3. Fulfill His plans for a person's life at any age. (Gen 17:16, Exodus 7:7)

©2005, dcg/atg.

Stages of Core Identity Development

"For I know the plans I have for you," says the Lord, plans for good and not for evil. Plans to give you a future and a hope."
Jeremiah 29:11

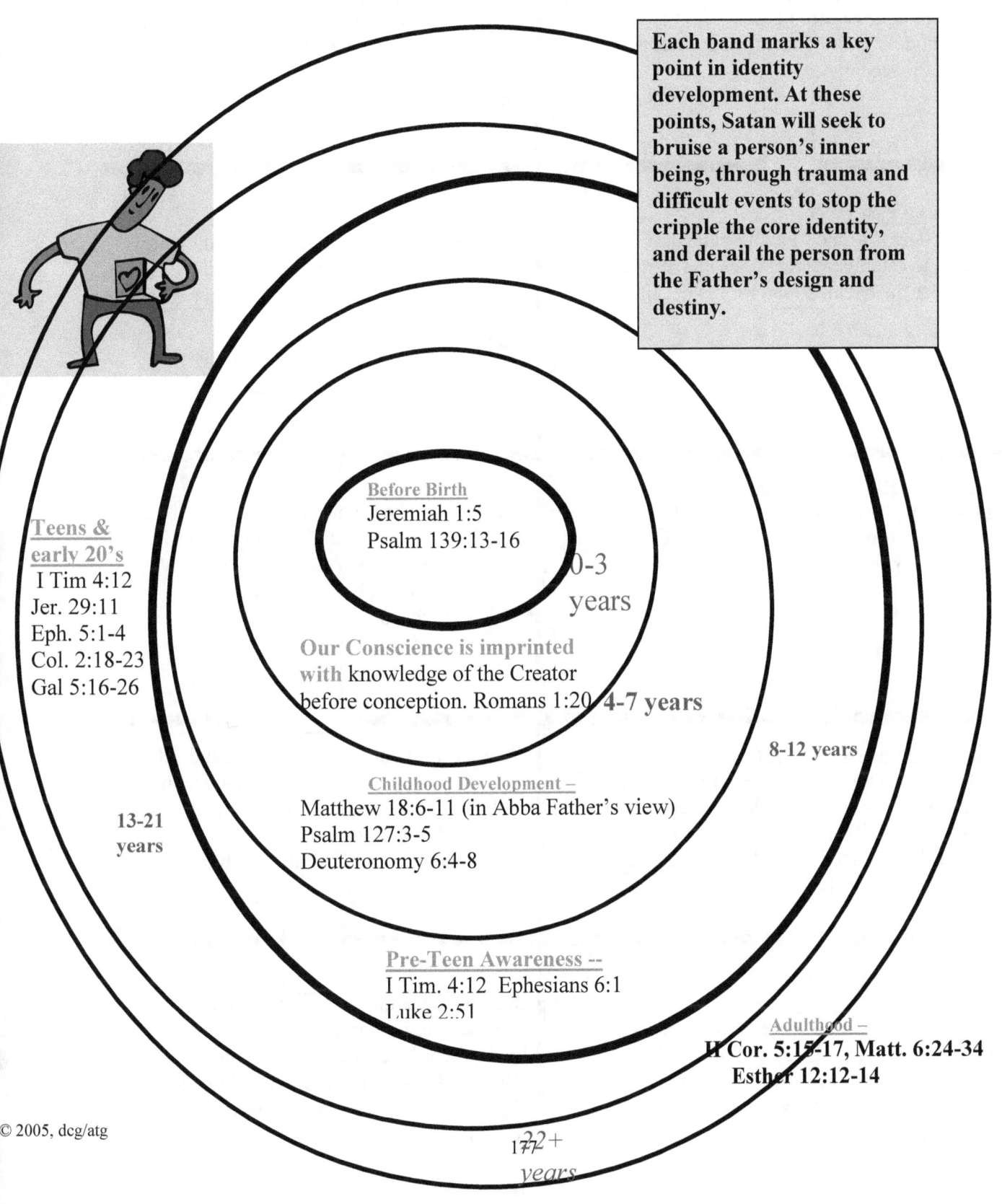

Each band marks a key point in identity development. At these points, Satan will seek to bruise a person's inner being, through trauma and difficult events to stop the cripple the core identity, and derail the person from the Father's design and destiny.

Before Birth
Jeremiah 1:5
Psalm 139:13-16

0-3 years

Our Conscience is imprinted with knowledge of the Creator before conception. Romans 1:20

4-7 years

8-12 years

Teens & early 20's
I Tim 4:12
Jer. 29:11
Eph. 5:1-4
Col. 2:18-23
Gal 5:16-26

Childhood Development –
Matthew 18:6-11 (in Abba Father's view)
Psalm 127:3-5
Deuteronomy 6:4-8

13-21 years

Pre-Teen Awareness --
I Tim. 4:12 Ephesians 6:1
Luke 2:51

Adulthood –
II Cor. 5:15-17, Matt. 6:24-34
Esther 12:12-14

22+ years

© 2005, dcg/atg

The Layers of Conformity

(Where am I currently living?)   *(The Corresponding Doorway Out)*

The Bondage of Conformity | The Power of Transformation

LAYER ONE
The person has a lack of inner identity formation Poor modeling, or no mentoring. Mental assent for acceptance.

"Father God, You created me. Jesus, You are the Source of My identity, and destiny. Holy Spirit, show me who I really am in You." I want everything in me to be born of the Spirit.

LAYER TWO
The person is afraid of man's rejection, and begins to establish perceptions and attitudes that alter the Created Plan for his/her life.

"Father, let me feel and understand your approval and blessing upon my life. It is my life's goal to walk in your Presence."
Matthew 6:5-8
Gal. 1:10

LAYER THREE – CONTROL and FEAR The person tries to conform to Codes of outward piety. This code of behavior Is inwardly focused.

"Father, show me your design for my life. I relinquish me right to rule my own life. I choose to allow You to dismantle my walls. I will receive Your love for me."
Matt 16:24-26
Rom. 8:15-16

LAYER FOUR - RELIGIOUS SPIRIT
The person seeks to create an environment according to perceived codes of piety. This code of behavior becomes more and more outwardly enforced upon the lives of others.

"Father, I repent for the attitudes and actions I have accommodated. I renounce the religious spirit, and its control, manipulation and pride. I choose to be a transparent vessel." Matt.23:24-28/18:1-10

LAYER FIVE—MASKS OF SPIRITUALITY
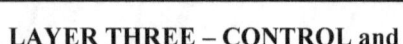
The person becomes entrenched in cyclic performance. Liturgical traditions. Rote responses. No heart activation. "Cold", "Desert," "Its for others, but not me."

Repentance. Admission of need for relationship. Discarding supposition of having heard it all before; becoming teachable. Willingness to step away from old patterns. The Holy Spirit activates the heart. Rom 5:5
Romans 14:17

The Walls of Self Protection and Pride

© 2005, dcg/atg

The Difference Between Conformity and Transformation

"I beseech you, therefore, brethren, by the mercies of God, that you present your bodies a living sacrifice; holy, acceptable God which is your reasonable service, and do not be conformed to rld, but be transformed by the renewing of your mind, that you may be able to prove what is that good and acceptable and perfect will of God." Rom. 12:1-2

Conformity	**Transformation**
(Mental focus – I.Q.)	(Heart focus (E.Q.)
Matthew 23:24:24-28	*Romans 8:12-18*
II Corinthians 11:3-4	*II Corinthians 4:1-6*
Fits into the mold	Inner identity formation
Outward expressions to earn acceptance	Inner understanding and relationship bring outward expressions
No deep feeling, or sense of flowing inner life	Inner joy and sense of contentment
Inner attitudes of criticism, judgmentalism,	Inner freedom, and personal accountability, Voluntary vulnerability
Intimidation forces order	Holy Spirit led order
Rule and Task oriented	Relationship oriented
Fear Motivated	Love and obedience motivation
Talks about God	Portrays life of Jesus, "Just shines"
Continually comparing self to others	Sense of personal destiny
Never good enough, Continually battles condemnation	Senses the approval and blessing of Father God, although imperfect
Strained to express heart in worship	Free and spontaneous worship
Invites religiousity, suspicion and Control into the life.	Holy Spirit guards the heart from Hell's attempts to suffocate the power of the
Becomes resistant to fresh patterns Of the Holy Spirit in the life of the believer	Holy Spirit in the life of the believer

The Difference Between Conformity and Transformation, cont'd

Conformity
(Mental focus – I.Q.)

Attitudinal Base of Operation

*"Everyone is the same – we must
all have the same likeness, or copy.
I must match others."*

The person has difficulty
getting an inner handle on
a deep purpose or direction for their life.

Conformity causes a "stretching out after,"
in which the person becomes larger in the
sense that they cover more area, but there is
no inner depth of emotional quotient, or
ability to relate beyond surface issues.
Tendency to defend past and compartmentalize
Pain.

Transformation
(Heart focus (E.Q.)

Attitudinal Base of Operation

*"Each person is precious and
unique; each with an irreplaceable
destiny and design."*

The person walks with inner purpose,
taking steps of obedience toward
a revealed/ intuitive purpose and
direction.

Transformation brings about a
"reaching upward and onward,"
in which the person becomes more
and more aware of the Presence of
Jesus on a daily basis. There is an
ever-increasing depth of worship and
vulnerability within the life. Pain
is brought into the light, and freedom
is the catalyst for further
development.

© 2005, atg/dcg.

Additional Notes and Discoveries:

If you discovered help and healing through <u>Ruth and Naomi – The Healing Journey,</u> you can find more of our ministry resources online at awakenedtogrow.com, on lulu.com, or amazon.com. Worship and devotional resources may also be found on iTunes.

Awakened to Grow Ministries
704-562-2897